C000094666

First published by H&H, 2013

Copyright © H&H, 2013
All rights reserved. This book, or parts thereof, may not
be reproduced in any form without permission.

H&H, Hesslewood Hall Business Park
Ferriby Road, Hessle, East Yorkshire, HU13 0LH

978-0-9926711-0-5

FOR MORE INFORMATION ABOUT
TOUGH AT THE TOP
01482 222 230
www.toughatthetopbook.com

TOUGH AT THE TOP

BY H&H

Contents

TOUGH AT THE TOP

BY H&H

Everyone has a dream, but only a lucky few of us have our dreams come true. Adam has always dreamed of owning a circus. But when he becomes the new ringmaster of the Starlight Circus, he has to contend with an anxious tiger-tamer, a frustrated carousel-owner, a delinquent trick-rider, a knife-thrower who hates his partner and a troupe of clowns who work strictly to rule…

Fortunately, Adam has a guardian angel in the shape of the Starlight Circus fortune-teller. Her wise advice helps him steer the circus from the brink of disaster towards an exciting new future.

The Dream

Everyone has a dream, but only a lucky few of us have our dreams come true. Adam's dream was to own a circus.

When Adam was five years old, his parents took him on an extravagant birthday trip to Paris to see the Starlight Circus. The bright brass notes of the band lit up the air, and the tigers blazed orange and black, and the Cossack riders had thick mustachios and horses even glossier than their boots. The clowns balanced perfectly between laughter and tragedy, and the trapeze artist was golden-brown and slender like a weasel, and Adam instantly lost his little-boy heart to her.

Adam said, "When I grow up, I'm going to own a circus just like this one and marry the girl who swung on the trapeze."

His parents laughed, but they took him to the fortune-teller's tent to have his palm read.

"Will I own a circus like this one day?" he asked the fortune-teller. "And will I marry the trapeze girl?"

"You won't marry the trapeze girl," the fortune-teller told him. "You're too young for her, and besides, she's already married. But if you work hard and stay honest and learn how to manage your inventory and keep an eye on your cash-flow, you will own a circus one day. Maybe even *this* circus."

Adam caught his breath in delight.

"And then," the fortune-teller continued, "you'll discover that everything you learnt about running a business isn't nearly enough. Because running a circus is all about knowing how to work with people."

"Are you really a fortune-teller?" Adam demanded. "Because my dad says fortune-tellers just make stuff up that they think you want to hear."

"We make dreams come true, you see." the fortune-teller continued, as if Adam hadn't spoken. "And if you want your circus acts to make other people's dreams happen, you have to understand their dreams too."

"Can I go now?" said Adam, who was, to be fair, only five.

"Yes, of course."

"Bye, then."

"See you in about thirty years," said the fortune-teller, waving.

Adam grew up, as small boys do. He worked in many different jobs – in a jam factory, on a fishing boat, as a night watchman at a sardine-canning plant, in the spoon division of a cutlery manufacturer (who sponsored his MBA) and finally in a management role at a soft-drinks company. But he never forgot his dream. When his work was hard or boring or he thought he might scream if he had to fill in just one more complicated spreadsheet, he gritted his teeth and reminded himself that one day, one day...

And then, for Adam, One Day finally arrived.

On a damp March evening thirty-one years later, Adam stood at the back of the line and waited to buy his ticket for the Starlight Circus's London performance. As the new ringmaster (as of midnight that night), of course he didn't have to pay, but he wanted to relive the excitement of passing through the ticket-booth and entering the Big Top.

The man on the ticket-booth was one of the off-duty clowns. He had a smear of greasepaint on his shirt and he didn't smile as he took Adam's money. Adam frowned, but the man wasn't looking at him. He was balancing a smartphone on his knee and was scrolling down his Facebook feed in between customers.

Well, that'll have to stop, for one thing, thought Adam to himself, and set off through the booths to buy himself some authentic circus snacks.

Somehow the circus wasn't quite as magical as he remembered it. The candy floss was sticky, and noticeably chewy towards the centre. The toffee on the toffee apples had flaked off in patches, leaving a disappointing object that was, frankly, little more than an anaemic-looking Golden Delicious on a stick. The staff holding open the entrance to the Big Top no longer swept off tall top hats as they bowed low. The painted horses on the carousel were missing their tails.

Adam took out a notepad and began to make notes. Then, remembering who he was, he hurried off to his caravan and put on his tight white jodhpurs and his scarlet tuxedo jacket and his tall, shining top-hat.

Although he couldn't take notes while he was in the ring, the list in his head grew longer as the performance unfolded. *Strongman not smiling at child before picking him up and carrying him round. Clowns visibly having massive argument in entrance to ring. Sea-lion tamer wearing jeans, not costume. Tiger act short by two, WHERE ARE THE OTHER TWO TIGERS? I KNOW I'M PAYING FOR THEIR KEEP. Elephants not painted. Magician not doing encore despite crowd calling for one. Sequins missing from trapeze girl's leotard. Trapeze catcher glared and audibly tutted when little boy asked mother very loudly if he could go to the toilet. Knife-thrower and knife-thrower assistant clearly hate each other [MUST CHECK H&S IMPLICATIONS ASAP]. Trick-diver platform too low, would look better diving from trapeze platform. Performance ran short —*

He checked his watch and realised that actually, no, it hadn't run short. In fact, it had run exactly to time.

The next day, he called a meeting at 9:30am, which was ridiculously early by Starlight Circus standards. The performers stood mutinously around in their jeans and sweatshirts, looking tired and dishevelled and ordinary. It was surprisingly difficult to catch their eyes.

"We need to talk about sharpening up our act," he announced.

Everyone stared back at him.

"Here's my list," he said proudly.

Everyone continued to stare at him.

"It's quite a long one," he warned them.

One of the clowns unwrapped a piece of chewing gum and put it in his mouth, in what felt to Adam like a needlessly aggressive manner.

"Let's talk about improvements," he said.

The strongman spat on the ground, then apologised. Adam was fairly sure he didn't mean it.

Adam read through his list. It took quite a long time and by the end, everyone was fidgeting.

"If you want me to put tails on the carousel horses I can do it," said the show-woman.

"Excellent, that's great -"

"But," she continued, "I'll need to close the ride for tonight while I do it."

"We can't afford to lose a night's revenue. Can't you do it during the day?"

"I've got plenty of other things to do during the day."

"But the ride looks a mess!"

"The horses don't need tails on them for the ride to go round and round," she pointed out. "It works fine just as it is. I did a steady business from the moment we opened. You'd have seen that if you'd been there all night, the way I was."

Adam thought of the golden horses that had haunted his dreams since he was a little boy. Their tails had streamed in the breeze and their nostrils had flared crimson. He'd closed his eyes and pretended his horse was real, that they were galloping into the sky. But who could believe in a horse without a tail?

"Is this going to take long?" asked the Tiger-tamer. "Only I need to get back and start their breakfasts."

"Their breakfasts?" Adam sighed. "Can't they wait?"

"They like their routine, do tigers," the Tiger-tamer said. "They get very upset if anything puts them out. And I'm not getting in a ring with upset tigers. It's not good for them. I had to keep two back last night as it was."

"Yes, I meant to ask you about that actually."

"We were ten minutes late going on," the Tiger-tamer explained.

"You can't have been, the show ran exactly on schedule."

"Ah, but the Cossack-riders wanted to be out by nine o'clock so they swapped with the Acrobats."

(Adam thought back. He vaguely remembered two people arriving in his caravan smelling of horses and sweat and gabbling out something about swapping round the order of the show. He had waved a munificent hand and told them it would be fine. He felt himself go pink.)

"You never asked me about it, you see," the Tamer continued patiently. "If I'd known in advance, I could have worked things out. But the Tigers don't like to be kept waiting. Once I've got them into the holding-pen, they have to be in the ring within three minutes or they get nervous. And you don't want a nervous tiger in the -"

"Yes, yes, I see. Well, we'll swap everything back for tonight, okay?"

"You can't!" A whippy teenager with an improbable black moustache stared at him in horror. "You said we could swap all week! I've got plans now!"

"Look, come and see me later and I'll see what I can work out, okay? We need to concentrate on the important stuff right now."

The boy looked as if he might cry. "But this is important!"

"*This* is important," Adam told them, waving his list.

"Why?" asked the clown with the chewing gum.

"Because we need to do better, that's why."

"What do you mean, *we need to do better?*" another clown demanded. (Adam vaguely recognised him as the one who always got the custard-pie in his face. When he looked more closely, he saw that there was an unattractive crust of old custard at the man's hairline.)

"We're doing all right, aren't we? We're selling tickets, aren't we? I didn't see any empty seats last night, did you?"

Adam remembered again the wild thrill of his first visit to the Starlight, and the anaemic taste of last night's toffee-apple.

"I came to this circus when I was five," said Adam.

"So?"

"So, it was magical!"

The custard-pie clown sniffed. "That's because *you were five.*"

"I know you're new and everything," said the man who ran the candy-floss stall. "But we've all been doing this for years. We know how to run it. My goodness, we could probably all do our jobs in our sleep now. Everything's fine."

"But if we stop trying to make things better -"

9

"I think you'll find," said the chewing gum clown smugly, "that we're all doing everything we're contracted to do. To the letter."

The Reality

Later that afternoon, Adam sat in his caravan and stared despairingly at the papers in front of him. The custard-pie clown (he would have to get to know their names at some point...it was so difficult to tell them apart without their costumes on) was right. Business was fine. They were booked solid for the next eighteen months, twenty-five days in each country, and then moving on in the darkness of the New Moon, as was traditional in the circus world. Ticket sales last night had been steady. Admittedly the queues hadn't started building hours before the doors opened, and some of the stalls had been quieter than he'd have liked, but –

He put on his coat and wandered outside.

After a few minutes he found himself outside the fortune-teller's caravan.

"Hello again," she said, as if Adam has just left her caravan a few days before.

She looked exactly the same as he remembered, which would have perplexed him if he had been less preoccupied with his own problems.

"You weren't at the meeting this morning," he said accusingly.

11

"No," she agreed.

"That's not on."

"Isn't it?"

"I'm the ringmaster now, you know. If I call a meeting then you should turn up to it."

"I'm not actually contracted to work for you before eleven o'clock," she said.

"Oh, not you as well," sighed Adam.

"Not me as well what?"

"Going on about contracted hours, and agreed duties, and keeping to agreements."

"I see," she said.

"They're driving me nuts," he said. "They all look so miserable!"

"Indeed."

"I mean, it's not like we're doing *badly* or anything," he said.

"That's true."

"People are still coming here."

"They are."

"I just – I just have this feeling, you know?"

"Yes?"

"A feeling like it's all going to go wrong any minute."

"Ah."

"But, I mean, you can't run a business based on feelings, can you?"

"If you say so."

"Business is about hard facts, not gut instinct. You can't go around worrying about whether people are happy or not. You have to look at the numbers. And the numbers are fine. Fine!"

"That's good to know."

"I mean, how much can it really matter if the horses haven't got any tails?"

"I'm sorry?" The fortune-teller looked startled.

"Oh, not the real horses. You know, the carousel horses."

"I see."

"I don't even know why I'm worried."

"Don't you?"

"Everything's fine," Adam said crossly, and got up and left without saying goodbye.

"See you soon," the fortune-teller called after him.

"Look," said Adam to the group of performers as they stood, shivering, in the centre of the Big Top on a rainy September Tuesday in Minsk, "we have to do something. We're selling fewer tickets at every stop. We're going to be bankrupt in two years."

The circle of blankly staring faces that looked back at him was not encouraging.

"We do everything we're supposed to do," said the Elephant Rider, playing with her thick black plait of hair.

"We turn up on time," said the trapeze artist.

"We have the right number of people on each stall," said the toffee-apple woman.

"And we rotate our stock properly," said the candy-floss man.

"We do our scheduled routines," said one of the clowns.

"We do encores whenever they wish for them," said the trick-diver.

"The ticket booth is always manned," said another clown.

"I wear my costume every night even though I absolutely hate it," said the can-can dancer.

"Yes," said Adam. "I know."

"If we put some more money in," said the candy-floss man hopefully, "we could hire some more people and get everything back the way it ought to be - "

"There isn't any more money!" Adam yelled. "That's the whole point! We can barely pay ourselves as it is! The last thing we need is more overhead!"

"So what do you want us to do?" a Cossack Rider asked him.

"I don't know," said Adam miserably, and turned away.

"Of course you know," said the fortune-teller, leaning out of her caravan as Adam went past.

"I'm sorry, what?"

"You know exactly what you want them all to do," she said.

"How – how did you know that – you weren't even at the meeting!"

"I'm a fortune-teller. I don't need to be at the meeting. Are you coming in for a cup of tea, or what?"

A few minutes later, Adam watched steam coiling from the spout of the large spotty teapot as the fortune-teller filled the mugs.

"What I want," he said, "is for them to work harder."

"No," said the fortune-teller. "That's not it."

"Yes, it is. I need them to do more or we're going to go broke in two years."

"About nine months, actually," the fortune-teller said. "But you're still not focusing on the right thing. You don't want them to work harder."

"But if they don't work harder, how are we going to get everything done?"

"What you need," said the fortune-teller, "is for them to care."

Adam was speechless.

"What you need," she continued, "is for them to care about the circus as much as you do. You need them to love what they do with all their heart. You need to remind them why they wanted to become performers in the first place. Once that happens, everything else is easy. What's the matter?"

"I shouldn't have to make them care," spluttered Adam. "Working here is their job!"

"Exactly. Their job. No more, and no less. But who gets excited about a job? What you want is for your people to feel like they're fulfilling their dreams."

Adam was astounded. "But – but – but – they get *paid*, don't they?"

"And does it look to you like that's enough? Or do you think you might need to help them love what they do for a living?"

"Look," said Adam, "I'm a busy man. I haven't got time to go round talking to people about how their day is and wondering if they're happy and all that stuff. I've got important things to do. I have to keep an eye on the cash-flow, I have to check the bookings, I have to monitor ticket sales - "

"Bookings and ticket sales, hmm? And how's that working out for you?"

"If I stop worrying about the numbers," said Adam, "what do you think's going to happen to us all? I'm here to manage the circus, not the people."

"So what is a circus, if it isn't the people?"

Adam opened his mouth, and then closed it again.

"I gave you a bit of advice a long time ago," said the fortune-teller, "but you were only five and I expect you've forgotten it by now. So, I'll tell you it again. I told you that running a circus is all about making dreams come true. Well, if you want your performers to make your customers' dreams come true, you have to do the same for them."

Adam stared at her for a minute, then, overcome with despair, put his head down on the table.

"I don't know how to do it," he said into the table-cloth. "I don't know a thing about that touchy-feely rubbish."

"You'll have to stop thinking of it as *touchy-feely rubbish* if you want to get anywhere," the fortune-teller warned.

"All right," said Adam meekly from the depths of the table-cloth. "What do I call it then?"

"Does it need to have a name? It's actually more of an attitude…a philosophy. It's about being genuinely interested in the wellbeing of others."

There was a pause.

"I'm not sure that I even understand what that means," Adam admitted.

"That's all right," said the fortune-teller. "I can help you."

"Um," said Adam, "I'm afraid I don't actually know, um…"

"My name?" The fortune-teller laughed. "You can call me Helen. Now, where do you want to start?"

The Vision Thing

During the busy, absorbed years when Adam had been working in what he had secretly thought of as his practice jobs, he'd never really seen the point of company visions. He'd been aware of them, of course – on posters in reception areas, on pocket-sized cards handed out to employees, at the start of important presentations – but until now he had never really felt the need for them. In his head, they had belonged in the category of *harmless but worthless*; things you had to brighten up the office and fill up an empty space on the wall, but which didn't add a lot of value, like doilies and pot-plants and pretty china.

Now, he found himself pacing the floor of his caravan and muttering to himself.

"What I need," he said, "is some sort of big idea. Something to inspire everyone and remind them all why they're here. Something everyone can get behind. I think I need..."

"You need a vision," said Helen. She was pouring boiling water into the teapot as she spoke.

"How do you always know it's me?" asked Adam. "And how do you always know what I want?"

"Oh, you know," said Helen mysteriously. "You have your thing, and I have mine."

"I know you've been telling me since Berlin that I needed one," said Adam, looking slightly shame-faced.

"That's all right, you got there in the end. So, where have you got to so far?"

"Not very far," Adam admitted. He held up a notepad, which was covered with scribbled words and crossed-out phrases.

"What do you think?" he asked.

"I think you might need to get some help," said Helen diplomatically. "Creating a vision isn't something you're meant to do all on your own. Have you talked to any of your performers about this?"

"My performers? God, no. This is strategic, not operational. Why would I want to talk to them?"

"Well, it is meant to inspire them, you know."

"Oh, they've all got plenty to be getting on with," said Adam bitterly. "In fact, that's all I ever hear from them – *I'm really busy just now* and *but this is how we've always done it* and *I don't think this is the right time to be making changes* and *I haven't got time*. It's driving me nuts. We're a circus! We're supposed to be exciting! Why aren't they more excited?"

"Maybe you ought to ask them," suggested Helen.

Adam wasn't listening.

"Besides," he said. "I tried that. Talking to them, I mean. It was a disaster. I had a meeting."

"Just the one?"

"Trust me, one was enough." Adam shuddered, remembering his disastrous attempt at team-building in those early days when he'd just taken over. "It was painful. Like walking over hot coals."

"Or wading through treacle," Helen suggested.

"Sorry?"

"Like you'd had to drag them all there, and every single second was an effort?"

"Yes," said Adam. "Yes, that's exactly it. It was completely hideous. There's no point talking to them – they're obviously not ready for it. I'll wait until I've got the vision. Maybe that'll get them feeling more enthusiastic."

"You know," said Helen, "it might be a good idea to do some listening for a change. Incorporate their thoughts into creating the vision."

"Oh, yes," said Adam, "that's a brilliant idea. *Working in a completely dysfunctional and jobsworth manner, we'll scrape along the bottom of the barrel and deliver a completely average circus experience to ever-decreasing crowds of unimpressed parents and disappointed children.* What?"

"So you have been listening," said Helen, looking amused. "Don't you find it interesting that, when you have to describe how things are right now, you can produce all of that straight off the top of your head, just from listening to your people? I wonder what would happen if you asked them all how they'd *like* it to be?" Adam looked at her blankly. "Never mind. You can try it your way if you like, I don't think you'll do too much damage. Just bear in mind I'll always be here whenever you need to talk."

Several weeks later, Adam emerged from his caravan into a damp Kiev afternoon, wild-eyed and inky and triumphant.

"I've done it!" he announced to the world at large.

He waited hopefully, but there were no curious heads peering over caravan doors or around corners. The rain continued to fall in the same fine mizzling mist that had enveloped them since they arrived.

"I've done it," he repeated, staring around.

The world maintained a polite silence.

"Never mind," he said to himself, and went back inside to look at the posters again.

Adam knew it wasn't good manners to admire your own work, but in his secret heart, he thought the vision looked pretty fantastic. A large, inspiring shot of the Big Top (artfully touched up to conceal the rain-streaks and the stains and the holes in the canvas), and, standing in front of it, Adam himself in his Ringmaster's outfit. He'd felt absurdly self-conscious being photographed, but he had to admit, the finished result was outstanding. And underneath, the words he'd slaved over:

"WHEN WE WORK TOGETHER, MAGIC HAPPENS"

He'd had a whole set of the posters printed, crisp inks on heavy paper, one for each performer. To accompany them, he'd chosen a series of inspiring posters that he felt illustrated important concepts for them all to get behind:

"TEAMWORK – *The fuel that lets common people deliver uncommon results"*

*"**COMMITMENT** – Winners don't just have goals. They have the need to achieve them"*

*"**CHALLENGE** – Climb as high as your dreams"*

*"**ADVERSITY** – It's just a stop on the road to success"*

*"**CUSTOMERS** – they don't stop us from going about our business. They are our business"*

"This'll do it," he said to himself. This had to be the answer. Every business he knew had a few of these posters around the place, and now he'd have them too. How silly he'd been to think they were just there for decoration. They were important, of course they were!

Humming to himself, he set off on his delivery rounds.

He could feel the difference in the atmosphere as soon as he stepped out of his caravan. There was a snap and a hum in the air, a sense of excitement and shared purpose that lit up the night around him. He was impressed. He hadn't expected his posters to be so successful so quickly. Who knew that getting your employees inspired could be this easy?

Maybe I'm better at this people management thing than I thought, Adam reflected as he strolled around the circus, enjoying the bright eyes and excited whispers of the performers as they flitted among the crowds.

He saw the first poster on the wall of the carousel ticket-booth. *Excellent,* he thought. *They've even put them up around the place, this is brilliant - ! Hang on, I don't remember ordering that one, I'm sure all of mine were photographs…*

Somebody in the circus had obviously had a very busy and productive afternoon. The drawing was clean, simple, accurate and horrible. With a terrible idiot smile plastered across his face, there loomed Adam unleashing a whip across a group of miserable-looking circus performers. Underneath was a carefully lettered caption:

*"**DREAMS**. Nobody gives a damn about yours. Now get back to work!"*

Adam swallowed hard. With a heavy heart he walked over to the wall took out the pins and folded the poster meticulously into his pocket, being very careful to line up the edges and make the folds neat and crisp.

His hopes that this was a one-off impudence evaporated as soon as he looked up from his careful folding. There was another one –leering at him from the side of the tiger-cage, showing Adam with that same inane and horrible smile, now standing on the tails of the tigers. Beneath, the caption read:

*"**EXPERTS**. We're paying you so we're allowed to ignore your opinion."*

He found the third stuck to the wall of the horse-boxes:

*"**TRAINING**. If we wanted you to do a different job we'd have given you it in the first place."*

And another by the side of the clown's dressing-tent:

*"**OPPORTUNITY.** The word your boss uses when he means 'you do more and get paid less'"*

But it was the one at the performer's entrance of the Big Top that upset him the most. It showed Adam dressed in a gorilla costume and holding a bag with the word "peanuts" written on it. The caption read:

*"**SALARY.** You work for a monkey. What else did you expect?"*

Adam stared at that one for a very long time, thinking of how hard he'd tried to keep the circus afloat without firing anyone, and of the feed bills and venue fees he was constantly juggling, and of the salary he hadn't drawn for the last seven months to try and keep costs down. He was surprised to find he was quite close to tears.

But the audience were there for a show, and the show must go on.

He strode into the Ring, and led the entire performance on auto-pilot. Then he went back to his caravan, laid the posters out neatly on his table, climbed into bed without undressing and slept for seventeen hours.

When he woke up, it was to the scent of frying bacon. At his desk, Helen was setting out two crusty slabs of bread with what looked like half a pig sandwiched between them, and a glass of orange juice.

"Everything looks better after a bacon sandwich," she said before Adam could open his mouth. "Come and sit down. And not a word until you've eaten."

To Adam's surprise, the bacon sandwich helped. By the time he got to the end of it, he'd made the important transition from *heartbroken* to *righteously furious*. As soon as he'd washed his face and cleaned his teeth, he thought, he was going to –

"Don't you even think about it," said Helen, pushing him back down into his chair. "Never make important decisions when you're angry. Besides, you've got work to do. You need to stop thinking of all the reasons they're in the wrong, and start *listening*."

"But – I mean, why couldn't they just come and talk to me about all this?" Adam demanded, gesturing to the hateful, hurtful pile of posters. "I suppose if that's how they really feel – but why not tell me? Is that too much to ask? Am I such a terrible boss?"

"Adam, look at the posters. They *are* telling you. They're telling you everything you need to fix to get this place back on track."

Adam looked mutinous.

"Well, it's a terrible way to get their point across."

"It's how you talked to them."

"But – but that was totally different - !"

"And the whole atmosphere was different last night – couldn't you feel it? They were all united."

"United in their hatred of me, you mean."

"And now you have to do something really tough. You have to go out there and make them *not hate you any more*. You have to take all that energy and direct it into something positive."

Adam blinked.

"And I got you something to help you," she added, and held out a zippered suit-bag.

The little collecting-ring at the back of the Big Top was crammed with performers. There was an angry electric buzz in the air, as if someone had stirred a beehive with a stick. *Helen's right*, thought Adam in surprise. *They are united. Just not in a very productive way, that's all. But I suppose that's my job…*

He took a deep breath, and strode into the collecting-ring. There was an audible gasp, and a few giggles, followed by a satisfying silence. Then, reluctantly, a scattering of applause and even a few respectful nods.

"Okay," said Adam, once everyone had had a chance to take in the sight of him in his gorilla-suit. "This is me, showing you that I'm listening. I understand now. I understand that you're scared and angry and unhappy. I know that things are bad. And I know I said I was going to make things better, and I know they've only got worse."

("Finally, some sense," muttered one of the clowns sarcastically. The other performers, however, were looking thoughtful.)

"The thing is," said Adam, "I've got some hope now." (Startled expressions.) "Because you've just shown me that actually, we can get ourselves out of the hole after all…" (Disbelieving looks, a few eye-rolls.) "I know because of these posters." (Blushes, awkward shuffles, mutters.) "Look at how much work went into them. It took me weeks to do mine. You did yours in a single afternoon! You must have all worked your socks off to get them ready." (A few guilty laughs.) "Now imagine if we put all that effort and energy into making the circus better. Imagine if we were working together, not against each other. *That's* why I know we can do it."

"What about salaries?" demanded a voice from the back.

"I know," said Adam, forcing himself not to look down at his feet. "I know we're behind on salaries. And as soon as we can, we'll fix it. That can't be right now, and we all know why. At the moment, we're barely breaking even."

This was the pivotal moment, the point where he could tip it either way. He took a deep breath.

"But let's be honest," he said slowly. "None of us are ever going to be rich by working here, are we? And if we wanted a steady pay-check and a three-bedroom semi in Basildon, we'd have chosen different careers. We didn't join the circus for the money. We joined it because it was what we dreamed of our whole lives."

(Was this working? At least they weren't throwing things…)

"I know we haven't spent much time working on everyone's dreams recently. I've been on everyone's backs about cost-saving and overtime and fixing things on the cheap. But I promise, I'm going to spend all my time now on finding out how we can make this a better place to work. Because a circus is about making dreams come true, and if yours aren't coming true for you, how can we make that happen for our audiences?" (He was sweating in the gorilla-suit and he knew his cheeks were flushed, but he couldn't worry about that now.) "Besides, I don't know about you, but I've had a rotten time the last seven months." (Murmurs of agreement.) "So what do we think? Shall we stop bickering and start dreaming?"

He hardly dared to breathe as he looked around at all the performers. To his utter shock, the slow murmur of agreement began to build into a spontaneous round of scattered applause.

There were still plenty of mutinous faces in the crowd. They were still two pennies from broke, the carousel horses still had no tails, the candy-floss machine still needed repairing and the Chief Clown was still looking at him with the cold, dead-eyed stare of a predator. He wasn't home-free yet.

But for the first time in months, he felt as if they were all on the same team.

"Thanks," he said, feeling awkward. "So, um – actually, I think I'll just…"

He began to struggle out of his gorilla-suit. Shreds of artificial fur clung to his white jodhpurs. He brushed them off impatiently, and reached for his top-hat.

Above their heads, the buzzer rang.

"Showtime," he said. "Everyone ready? Then let's go."

The Cossack Riders

Adam first noticed the man because of his clothes. Standing out because of your clothes took some doing in a world where grown adults routinely put on giant shoes, scarlet wigs and whitefaces, and where men and women alike wore sequins and magenta lycra without the slightest embarrassment. Nevertheless, the man's alligator cowboy boots, black leather duster, handlebar moustache and battered ten-gallon hat caught Adam's eye one near-freezing November evening in Budapest. The man had a ringside seat, and - judging by the way the men on either side of him had carefully left room between them - he had come to the circus alone. He sat quietly, applauded politely, ate a small cone of popcorn and folded the wrapper into his pocket.

Then the Cossack riders came on, and he sat bolt upright and studied every moment of the act as if there would be a test afterwards.

Of course, Adam thought to himself, that might just be because he wanted to see how securely the female members of the Cossack team were laced into their costumes. A lot of bored fathers became noticeably more cheerful during the Cossack act, in the same way a number of mothers took an intense and slightly predatory interest in the Trapeze team.

Still, it was odd that the man in the ten-gallon hat turned up to every one of their Budapest performances, night in, night out.

They moved on to Vienna, then Salzburg, and Adam forgot about him for a while. Then in Munich, on their first night, the man in the cowboy hat was there again. The same ringside spot, the same black duster, the same-sized cone of popcorn – and the same consuming interest in the Cossack team.

Of course, the circus world had always attracted its fanatics. Even these days, the Starlight Circus had a few compulsive followers. Some had impractical dreams of joining the team. Others simply adored the tawdry romance of it all (*rather more tawdry than romance at the moment,* thought Adam grimly, remembering the receipts from Salzburg and wincing). But the cowboy didn't seem to fit either of these categories. He wasn't keen enough, for one thing. He didn't laugh at the clowns in that slightly ostentatious, I-appreciate-this-at-a-deeper-level-than-you manner. He didn't nod knowledgeably during the knife-throwing. He didn't even try to look up the skirts of the dancing girls.

But every time the Cossack team galloped in, he sat ramrod-straight and stared intently, not moving, barely blinking.

It was very strange. But Adam had a lot of other things to think about, so he put it to the back of his mind as one of the inexplicable mysteries life throws at you sometimes.

Then one afternoon, he glanced out of his window at the thin Munich sunshine and saw the man in the long black leather duster making his way between the caravans. He was heading in the direction of the stables.

Adam's initial plan was to somehow sneak across the showground without being noticed by the man in the black leather duster. After twenty yards of keeping to the shadows and scuttling across patches of empty ground, he glimpsed the astonished face of the candy-floss man peering through his kitchen window, and realised how absurd this must look to anyone who *wasn't* the man in the leather duster. *Besides,* he thought crossly, *this is my bloody circus, not his. I'll just go over there and ask him what on earth he thinks he's doing here...no! No, that's not on, he's a customer after all, I can't be rude to him. I'll just wander casually over and ask him what he's doing here.*

Trying to remember how his arms were supposed to move when he walked casually took quite a while. Adam finally made it over to the stables just in time to see the man in the duster shaking hands with the youngest Cossack rider and walking away. Adam hadn't learned the Cossack riders' names yet; but he recognised the boy because it always looked so odd to see a young man not yet out of his teens ride into the ring wearing the traditional waxed moustache of the trick-rider. (If he was honest, he had also been somewhat envious of the boy's facial-hair-growing skills. Adam himself, fair-haired and pale-skinned, had barely needed to shave before the age of twenty-five. It had come as something of a relief to discover that the boy glued his moustache on before the performances.)

The boy wasn't wearing his moustache this afternoon. However, he was wearing a look of beatific disbelief, as if he had just been handed the winning lottery-ticket by his guardian angel.

"Hello," said Adam; a safe conversational opener.

"It's amazing," said the boy.

"Um - is it?"

"The most incredible thing just happened to me," said the boy, rubbing his hands over his flushed cheeks. "That man – that man I was just talking to."

"Yes?" said Adam, thinking this was going to be easier than he thought.

"He came to offer me a job."

"You've got a job." Adam was instantly on the defensive. The Cossack riders were a tight-knit team. More than that, they were a *good* tight-knit team, consistent and competent and dependable. Their act had the smooth mechanical perfection of a clockwork toy. The last thing he wanted was for anyone to start messing with their heads by tempting one of their number away.

"He's setting up a new act," said the boy. "He's from Texas."

"Oh, really? Because I would have guessed Baltimore."

"He worked at a rodeo," said the boy, ignoring Adam's sarcasm. "They do all sorts of different things over there - they use different saddles and they train their horses differently as well, they have more Mustang blood in them so they're -"

"He wants you to go to America?" asked Adam.

"Oh, no," said the boy.

"Well, thank God for that."

"He's looking at developing a Rodeo circuit in Europe," said the boy. "He can't afford fixed venues yet so he wants a travelling team." His eyes were dazed and radiant. "And he asked me. He said I've got a real talent."

Adam felt as if he was trapped in a nightmare. The Cossack act was built on symmetry. They had to have four pairs of riders for the performance to work. If he lost this boy Adam thought to himself, the whole act would fall apart -

"Only he needs me to be ready to go in two weeks."

Suddenly the nightmare appeared to have an end-point.

"Well, that's no good to you, I'm afraid, then," said Adam cheerfully. "You're on three months' notice. Sorry," he added, seeing the boy's face.

"He won't wait. He needs me in two weeks. Please, can't you just -"

"I know it's tough, but I can't afford to lose you with no notice. It's three months for a reason. Good riders aren't easy to find, you know. And good riders who are happy to travel – well, trust me, if I find one even in three months, I'll be lucky. To be honest, I'm doing you all a favour by *only* asking for three months. Besides, everyone else is depending on you. You've got to remember, we're all part of a team."

"I've been in the team for three years," said the boy. "I've been riding in the same spot all that time."

"And that's why you're so good," said Adam encouragingly. "You've got the slickest act in the whole circus. It runs like clockwork. It's about the only time in the whole night when I know I can relax."

"But I'm bored!" yelled the boy. "I'm nineteen years old and I'm bored out of my mind. I don't want to do the same routine every night of my life and wait for someone else to retire before I ever get to try something new. What's the point?"

"You're a really important member of the act," said Adam. "Doesn't that make you feel good?"

"On the rodeo circuit," said the boy, "the riders have competitions to see who can come up with the best new trick of the season."

"We just can't afford to lose you right now," said Adam. "You're too important to lose. Are you – are you crying?"

"Of course I'm not crying," said the boy furiously, stalking away.

"It's just not fair," said Adam to Helen, taking the mug of tea and sitting down in the chair she offered him. "Why did it have to be one of the Cossack riders? They're the best act I've got."

"And that's exactly why he wants José. Nobody headhunts your *bad* performers, do they? Take it as a compliment. Losing people is a pain, but it's got to be better than having badly-trained idiots no-one else would want to employ."

He put his mug down on the table. "Do you know how long it'll take to find a Cossack rider?"

"No, but I'm glad to hear you do. Tell me."

"Months," said Adam gloomily. "Months and months and months. Miguel's really picky. And when you've got them, it takes hours of practice for them to get ready. And it unsettles all the other horses while you're waiting. Three months' notice is *generous* under the circumstances." He'd been trying to ignore the plate of biscuits, but the siren call of the custard creams was simply too much to resist. "It's not fair."

"No, it's not fair at all."

"All that time and effort that's gone into training him, and now he wants to just clear off to some poxy rodeo outfit!" Adam dunked his biscuit into his tea. "At least you agree with me."

"Oh, I don't agree with you in the slightest," said Helen. "I just said it wasn't fair."

Adam looked at her blankly.

"I mean," she went on, "it's not fair *to José*."

"Not fair to José? Not fair to hold someone to their notice period? Not fair to think of the impact on the rest of the team?" Adam was astounded. "How am I not being fair?"

"Because you promised to start trying to make their dreams come true," said Helen. "José told you he wants to become a brilliant trick-rider and progress his career. And you just stamped all over it."

Adam's custard-cream had disintegrated into his tea. He fished hopefully around with the teaspoon, but it was a lost cause.

"Look," he said, "when I said I wanted to make their dreams come true, I didn't -"

"Mean it?"

"No no no, of course I meant it, but I just didn't think it would involve, you know, involve, involve - "

"Yes?"

"I thought it might be a bit easier than this," Adam admitted reluctantly, taking another custard cream. "I just – I thought everyone else would have the same dream as me, you know? Or at least similar."

"If they had exactly the same dream as you, they'd all be after your job," said Helen. "Be glad they all want different things."

Adam ate his biscuit crossly.

"So what are you going to do?" asked Helen, watching him with bird-bright eyes.

"You think I should let José go, don't you?" said Adam in disbelief.

"I do."

"But – but that'll upset everyone else on the Cossack team!"

"If you don't handle it properly, then yes; that's exactly what will happen."

"And that's good management, is it? Giving one unhappy employee everything he wants, and making everyone he works with wonder why they bother trying to do a good job every day?"

"Or," said Helen, "you could stop complaining, and start working on a solution."

Adam looked at her reproachfully.

"Have you ever heard of the *zero sum game*?" Helen asked.

"Of course," said Adam.

"Describe it for me?"

"It's – well, it's a way of expressing the idea that your gain is always balanced by someone else's loss. Like, if I have a pie and you want half of it, then I've only got half the amount of pie I had before. Because there's only so much pie to go round."

"And is that how you're seeing the situation with José?"

"Well, of course it is," said Adam, after a confused pause. "How else can I possibly look at it? There's only so much José to go round. If I let him go in two weeks, then in two weeks I'm short of one Cossack rider."

"Rubbish," said Helen briskly. "You're not managing time, you're managing happiness. Happiness is not a pie. When it comes to managing your team, happiness is a potentially infinite resource. You just need to find out how to make more of it to help solve this situation."

"Can I possibly have that in English?" asked Adam, after another confused pause.

Helen smiled.

"Of course. Here's what I think you should do…"

The cowboy's name, it turned out, was Reuben Jackson. His handshake was firm, he drank the coffee Adam offered him without noticeably wincing, and his long, incomprehensible, horse-based conversation with head Cossack rider Miguel seemed immensely satisfying to both of them. Adam poured more coffee, offered round the biscuits, and waited for the conversation to turn to subjects he understood.

"I'm sorry," said Reuben at last, turning to Adam. "When you put two horse people together, we become just about the biggest bores in the world."

"Not at all," said Adam politely. "It was very interesting."

Reuben grinned. "Now, that's real nice of you, Adam, but I finally learned *interesting's* what you Brits say when you want to be polite about something you hate. Let's talk about your boy José, shall we?"

"He's good," said Miguel proudly.

"He surely is. Six months with me and he'll be even better. Wish I had twenty that good in my sights."

"Good people are hard to find," said Adam, trying to sound sympathetic through gritted teeth.

"Ain't that the truth. I got them queuing out the door to try, mind you. Drives me nuts. I get all excited to see them ride, and then…I got a whole bunch of them about halfway there – back home I'd take 'em on and break 'em in. But I ain't got no *depth*, you know? I need a team that's ready to go now, not halfway from next Octember. Now you guys -" he nodded at Miguel – "you've got the kind of set-up I want to build. You got your bright young things and your steady old hands. You can train your talent. Me, I got to buy it in at god-damned premium rates."

Adam's immediate impulse was to remind everyone at the table that Miguel, like José, had signed a contract with a three-month notice period, but he clenched his fists under the table and managed to restrain himself.

"Ah, but in the rodeo you have individuality," said Miguel, sounding wistful. "And always the new blood to train! Sometimes I wonder…"

The words *Don't you dare try and poach my Cossack team* were right on the edge of Adam's tongue. If he opened his mouth they would flop out onto the table, floundering around and wrecking everything. *Happiness is not a pie,* he repeated to himself, as if that was going to help. *Happiness is not a pie. José and Miguel are not pies. That's ridiculous though – that's exactly what they're like. And where am I going to get another rider to train with just two weeks' notice? And even if I find one, what's the point if they're just going to leave as soon as they're trained –*

Oh, thought Adam, slightly shamefaced.

"Did you say," he said slowly, "that you had a lot of kids who need training?"

"This will be fantastic," said Miguel, rubbing his hands together. "Fantastic!" His eyes were bright. "It's time our team had some new blood."

"And you're sure you're happy to train two new apprentices every year?" Adam repeated anxiously.

"Of course!"

"And the exchange programme? You don't mind swapping one of your crew for a rodeo rider?"

"Do I *mind*?" Miguel laughed.

"But what about your team, won't they -"

"They will fight for it," said Miguel firmly. "And the horses will be pleased too. They like to learn new things."

"You know," said Adam, "I thought your team were happy as they were. The act's so perfect, you see."

"Perfection is boring," Miguel declared grandly. "The essence of horseback-riding is unpredictability. Otherwise, we would ride motorbikes."

"That sounds a bit alarming actually," said Adam. "Like you're all going to be falling off the whole time and making a mess of things." Miguel laughed. "Okay, really not helping."

"Perhaps one or two falls. How else do we learn?"

Adam remembered the smooth, mechanical perfection of the Cossack routine, and sighed. "I thought you already knew everything you needed to know?"

"No-one ever knows everything they need to know."

"I suppose not," Adam admitted.

Miguel clapped Adam on the shoulder.

"It will be splendid," he said.

The Cleaner

It took Adam a long time to notice it, partly because we rarely notice things that consistently and reliably *aren't* there, and mainly because he was so busy with everything else. But one cold day in March, it dawned on him. He was walking round the back of the Big Top in the slanting golden Prague sunlight, when a solitary popcorn cone tumbled joyously across the frozen ground and gambolled around his feet.

He picked it up and stared at it in perplexity.

Last night, the circus had sold four thousand six hundred and nine cones of popcorn. By the time the iron gates finally swung shut, the visitors had consumed five thousand four hundred and twenty-eight clouds of candy-floss. Three thousand five hundred and ninety hot-dogs (two thousand and seven with onions) had been wolfed hungrily down. One thousand four hundred and seventy toffee-apples had been unwrapped and sucked clean by one thousand four hundred and seventy sticky children.

Then, this morning…one solitary popcorn cone.

At that moment, a small mousey man came round the corner with a heavy-duty plastic garbage-bag and a spike.

"Oh," he said, looking at the popcorn cone in Adam's hand. "I'm sorry. May I?"

Adam handed over the popcorn cone. The man twinkled it away into the garbage-bag and shuffled quietly away again.

"Wait a minute," said Adam. "Can I talk to you for a bit?"

The man glanced at his watch.

"Ah. If you're going off-duty, I can catch you later."

"Oh, no, it's not that," he said. "It's just that Dmitri started cleaning out the tigers half an hour ago and I like to get their bedding and such safely out of the way before Shauna brings the horses out. They've got a new routine to practice, and the smell of tiger-scat frightens them, you see. But I can talk to you while I work if that's any good?"

"Yes, of course, that's fine," said Adam, and followed the mousey man through the brightly-striped canvas panels that concealed the working life of the circus from its visitors.

In the empty tiger-cage, the smell of tigers was pungent. As discreetly as possible, Adam pulled his sleeve over his hand and covered his nose.

"Do you have a team then?" he asked.

"Oh no." The cleaner smiled. "Just me."

Adam remembered the (rather small) line in his overhead sheet which covered *Cleaning services. No,* he thought, *we're barely paying enough for one person, never mind a whole team.*

"And where are the tigers now?" he asked.

"Gone for a swim," said the cleaner.

"Er – did you just say they'd gone for a swim?"

"Dmitri was worried," said the cleaner. "They like water, you see. And that's hard to organise when we're on the move. But then I remembered Marcel's tub. I asked Mick and Rommel, the strongmen you know, to carry it out to their outdoor enclosure after Marcel finishes his dive practice. Apparently carrying unstable loads is good for stamina and endurance, so they don't mind doing it. Then in the morning, Dmitri takes the tigers for a swim while I clean out their cage, and then after they've finished playing, I clean the tub out. So everyone's happy."

"Huh," said Adam, astonished.

"What did you want to ask me about?" the cleaner asked, busily filling garbage-bags.

Adam's original plan had been to ask the cleaner how it was that, of all the many functions in the circus, the one he would have imagined was the least glamorous and exciting was somehow the one that operated the most perfectly. But he had just had a far more thrilling idea.

"I'm going to promote you," he said recklessly. "You know everything there is to know about this place. You're just who I've been looking for."

"I'm sorry?" The man looked horrified.

"I said I'm going to promote you," said Adam, not noticing the man's expression. "You'll be my personal assistant."

"But I don't want to be your personal assistant."

"Oh, no, it's not what you're thinking," said Adam. "You won't be like my secretary or anything, I don't expect you to make me tea or organise my diary."

"No, really. Thank you, but no. I don't want a new job. I'm happy in the job I've got."

"You'll get to really use your talents properly at last," said Adam. "All the stuff you know about everyone, all the people-management side of it, getting the logistics organised better so people enjoy what they're doing. You'll be magnificent."

"I thought I was doing a pretty good job of what I'm doing now," said the man, looking hurt.

"Of course you are! You're the only thing in this whole place that works properly."

"Then why are you trying to make me stop?"

"I'm not trying to make you stop," said Adam, bewildered. "I'm trying to reward you for the amazing job you're doing by giving you a new, more interesting job that you'll really enjoy."

"I like cleaning."

"Rubbish, no-one likes cleaning. We'll just get in some minimum-wage chimp to replace you, and -"

"Excuse me," said the little man, suddenly fierce, "but how dare you?"

Adam shrank back from the sharp rubbish-spike that was suddenly being waved under his nose.

"I didn't mean to upset you," Adam said.

"Well, you have."

"I realise you'll need some time to think about it."

"I don't want a new job!" the man said desperately. "Please don't try and give me one."

"Look, just think about it, okay?" said Adam.

"I had a breakthrough this morning," said Adam to Helen, over a large mug of tea.

"Oh, yes?"

"Yes. I found this fantastic guy - the cleaner actually. He's been doing a brilliant job, knows everything there is to know about how this place works. He's wasted in his current role."

"Niall? I hope you didn't tell him that," said Helen.

"Of course I did! He's got so much more to offer the world than what he's doing now. It's a great opportunity to everyone. I've offered him a promotion."

"I see," said Helen. "And how did he react?"

Adam looked shifty.

"Well, he was a bit overwhelmed, naturally."

"Are you saying *overwhelmed* when what you really mean is *angry*?"

"I wish you wouldn't do that," said Adam.

"And I wish you'd listen to what people tell you occasionally," said Helen, sighing.

"What are you talking about?"

"It's like this," said Helen. "Since you were five years old, you've wanted to own a circus. Right?"

"Yes."

"So, in spite of everything – all the worry and the late nights and the people problems - the job you're doing right now is your dream job, yes?"

"You know it is," said Adam. "But I don't see what this has got to do with anything."

"Supposing someone came and offered to buy the circus off you and put you in charge of running a huge multinational company worth squillions? What would you say?"

"I'd say no, of course."

"But what if they insisted? What if they said it was all for your own good, and you were wasted running a circus anyway, and then they snuck in one night and bought it without you knowing anything about it?"

"You know, that couldn't actually happen," said Adam.

"Use your imagination," said Helen. "Okay? Are you imagining that now? Yes? Good. Now you have to go and work for the huge multinational. Except that, the next day, someone from *another* circus comes along and asks you to come and work for *their* circus instead..."

"But my job's a proper job!" said Adam. "It's a calling. It's my dream. Nobody dreams about being a cleaner."

"You mean *you* never dreamed about being a cleaner," said Helen. "And you know what? I never dreamed about wanting to own a circus. What on earth makes you think everyone has the same dream?"

"But anyone can be a cleaner!" said Adam in despair. "He's got real talent! I can't stand seeing talent going to waste."

Helen sighed.

I tell you what," she said. "I'll make a deal with you. You go and try your hand at the cleaner's job for a day. Just one day. Starting tonight when the gates open. Rodrigo can stand in for you in the Ring just for one night – he's dying to give it a go. And if at the end of the night, you still think you want to make the cleaner into your assistant and hire a minimum-wage chimp to do his work, then I'll help you talk him into it."

"I have to go and be a cleaner for a night, and then I get my assistant?"

"That's one way of looking at it," said Helen cautiously.

"Okay, then," said Adam. "It's a deal."

As the gates to the circus opened, Adam stood beside the cleaner clutching his rubbish-spike like a talisman and feeling strangely excited.. The line outside the gates wasn't as long as he'd have liked, but it was still longer than it had been a few months ago, which made him feel cautiously happy. A little boy rummaged through his pocket, and a scrap of paper fluttered down to the ground.

"I'll get that," said Adam, leaping forward. He stabbed eagerly with his rubbish-spike, and missed. He stabbed again, and missed again, but bumped into the child's father, who looked at him angrily. "Sorry," said Adam, stabbing again. This time he got the tip of the spike through the father's shoelace.

"Look," said the father, "do you have to do this right now? It's all right," he added to his son, whose bottom lip had begun to quiver, "it's just a bit of sweet-wrapper, they know you didn't do it on purpose."

The child's mother picked up the sweet-wrapper and handed it to Adam with icy politeness.

"I'm sorry," said Adam, horrified. He slunk back to where the cleaning man was watching with a slight smile on his face.

"I made a little boy cry," he confessed.

"You didn't mean to."

"I know," said Adam. "I was only trying to pick up the litter. But I still did it." He shook his head. "You keep this place immaculate. How do you do it if you don't keep on top of it like that?"

"Maybe wait until they've all gone in," the cleaner said.

"But won't they'll tread it all into the ground?"

"That's why we've got spikes. Besides, they're here to have fun. You don't want to be treating them like naughty children, do you?"

The cleaner waited until the crowd had passed by, then sidled quietly forward and began impaling rubbish with one quick flick of his pike. Trailing discreetly in the wake of the crowd, he picked up scraps and bits and fragments, sliding them into his bag whenever his spike became too full. In a few minutes the ground was perfectly clear. Then he went to see how Adam was getting on.

Adam stood frowningly over an empty carton of raisins, jabbing at it with his spike. He couldn't seem to get the hang of impaling the rubbish without stabbing straight through into the ground as well.

"Like this," said the cleaner, spiking up the raisin-box with a quick flick of his wrist.

After the first fifty or so attempts, Adam finally mastered his impaling technique, and began spiking up popcorn boxes, napkins and the cellophane from toffee-apples with enthusiasm. What he struggled with was the delicate art of collecting the rubbish without upsetting the people around him. Again and again he found himself barging into people, tripping over feet, jostling startled toddlers in pushchairs, knocking over unexpected children.

After a while, recognising he was doing more harm than good with his attempts, he stood and held the rubbish-bag and watched in awe as the cleaner slid in and out of the crowd, unobtrusively collecting bits and scraps and cartons, never making contact, never interrupting, a meticulous delicate dance.

"How do you do that?" he demanded as the last customer disappeared into the Big Top and the heavy red velvet of the curtain fell behind them.

"I don't know, really." The cleaner shrugged. "Practice?"

"So what happens now?" asked Adam, whose feet were aching. "Do we stop for a break while the show's on?"

"Oh, that was just the first sweep," said the cleaner. "Now we go round and do it all again."

By the time the curtains fell on the Big Top, Adam thought he might scream if he ever saw another popcorn box or paper napkin again. His feet were on fire, his arms were stiff, he was cold, he was exhausted, and he knew that as soon as the crowd streamed out across the showground towards the exit, there would be a further tidal wave of litter in their wake. By the time he finally stumbled towards his caravan, he was barely able to summon the energy to raise his head. When he saw Helen's caravan door open and a mug of tea held out to him like bait, he was unable to resist.

"You look all in," Helen observed.

"Cleaning," said Adam, with feeling, "is harder than it looks."

"I thought it might be."

"Is that why you made me do it?"

"You're really starting to catch on," said Helen approvingly. "Now, tell me. What are you going to say to him tomorrow?"

Adam was waiting for the cleaner when he came round the corner of the tiger-cages. When he saw Adam, he stopped apprehensively.

"You were right," said Adam, before the cleaner could speak. "I'm sorry I was so rude before. Of course I can't just get any old fool off the streets to come in and do what you do. Cleaning is an incredibly difficult job."

"Thank you," said the cleaner.

"I never realised before," Adam continued, "just how much went into it. You make it look easy, but it's not. You only make it look easy because you've worked really hard to get good at it. And you are good at it. In fact, you're amazing. I think you must be the very best cleaner in the whole world."

The cleaner smiled.

"And because of that," said Adam, "I'd be absolutely mad to want to move you out of a job you love and that you're brilliant at. But I do very much want to hold on to you, for as long as I possibly can. So I'd like to give you a pay-rise."

"I'm already getting paid the standard rate for my job," the cleaner pointed out.

"Yes, I know. That's the whole point. I want to pay you more than the going rate because I really, really want to hold on to you and I want to make it as difficult as possible for other circuses to tempt you away.

"But I really don't want or need any more money," the cleaner insisted. "I'm pleased you've recognised the amount of effort and pride I put into my job. That'll do me nicely."

Adam relented, not wanting to spoil this moment with dogged determination.

"OK - but if you ever do think about leaving, I'd really like it if you'd come and talk to me first so I can see if there's anything we can work out."

The cleaner's smile made every moment Adam had spent picking up litter the night before worthwhile.

The Carousel

In the damp London air, Adam stood quietly beside the carousel ride and watched the little girl circling the roundabout. She was about six years old, her hair still soft and downy, her eyes big and bright. Her lips moved as she studied each horse in turn.

Adam knew exactly what she was doing. She was choosing the right horse, *her* horse, the horse she would pretend was real, the horse she'd take away into her dreams and ride all the way up to the stars.

Celestia. Rosie. Mickey. Argus. Josie. Marvin. Blue.

But none of the carousel horses caught her fancy. He watched the expression in her eyes as she went from excitement to disappointment to something verging on tragedy.

"I wanted to ride a horse with a *tail*," she whispered to her father, and he picked her up in his arms and carried her away.

That's it, thought Adam to himself, watching the little girl's head droop onto her father's shoulder. *I'm getting this carousel fixed if it's the last thing I do.*

Next morning, he went round to the carousel owner's caravan bright and early, determined not to let another day go by without some proper action being taken on the battered, tail-less horses. The carousel was a disgrace, he told himself. It was a disgrace where it should be a destination, a beacon, a nugget of pure childish joy.

Standing on the doorstep, a thought occurred to him. He climbed back down off the step and went round to see Niall the cleaner, who (he now knew) would be hosing down the crate that transported Roisin, the circus's much-pampered elephant.

"Niall," he asked, shame-faced, "the lady who runs the carousel – she's called Anna, yes?"

"Anne," said Niall, shovelling elephant-droppings into a bucket.

"Thanks," said Adam, and went back to the caravan.

Kind but firm, he thought to himself. *Kind but firm. Kind but firm. We have to get this sorted. Kind but –*

Before he could knock on the door, it opened and there was a tired-looking woman about his own age standing in the doorway.

"Hello," she said, without enthusiasm. "Have you got your shoes on yet?"

Adam glanced down at his feet.

"And get your books," she continued.

"I think you might have me confused with someone else -" Adam couldn't help feeling he had lost the conversational initiative.

"And give me a kiss," said the woman, outrageously. Adam blinked in shock, but then a boy, just stretching out from small-sized chubbiness into middle-sized ganagliness, dived under Anne's arm, held up a resigned face for her to press her lips to, glanced at Adam, shrugged, and scurried off between the caravans.

"Sorry about that," said Anne, although she didn't sound particularly sorry. In fact she didn't sound particularly anything. Her face was tired and dead-looking and her hair needed brushing. "What can I do for you?"

"I didn't know -" right on the edge of the social precipice, Adam realised that *I didn't know we had any children at the circus* was possibly not the very best thing he could say at that moment. "I mean, I wondered if I could have a word about the carousel."

"If you like," said Anne dully. "I'll have to get the washing-up done while we talk, though."

Adam thought about protesting that he needed her full attention, but for a moment he caught Anne's eye, and from the depths of her calm, polite, dead demeanour, he saw a glint of sheer fury that made him reconsider. He followed Anne into her caravan and waited to be told he could sit down.

Anne collected cups and plates from the tiny foldaway dining table and poured out boiling water from the old-fashioned kettle on the gas-ring.

"Is it okay if I sit down?" Adam asked at last.

"Of course," said Anne, somehow making this sound like the stupidest question anyone had ever asked.

Adam sat down on the long sofa, next to a pile of perfectly folded t-shirts, which he presumed must belong to her son. Anne picked up the pile of t-shirts and moved them six inches further away. Adam felt like a criminal.

"I hope I didn't crease them," he said.

Anne turned back to the washing-up bowl and squirted in a small, neat measure of Fairy liquid.

"I wanted to talk to you about the carousel," he began.

Anne's back stiffened slightly. She reached for the mop and began on the glass tumblers.

"It's a bit run-down," Adam said. This was a long way from describing his feelings of righteous outrage at the state of the carousel, but something told him he should tread carefully here.

Anne carefully stacked the glasses on the draining-rack, one next to another next to another, and began on the plates.

"I think it needs some work doing," he said.

Anne reached for the kettle and poured in a careful half-inch of extra hot water.

"The horses are in a total state," he said, wondering if Anne was going to remain entirely silent until he left the caravan again.

Anne reached for the frying-pan.

"Well," said Adam, feeling slightly desperate. "That's what I think, anyway. But, ha ha, what would I know anyway, right? I mean, I'd love to know what your thoughts are, Anne."

When Anne turned around, she was holding the mop like a weapon. However, her voice was perfectly calm and correct.

"My thoughts about what?" she asked.

"About the state of the carousel."

"I think you mentioned it when you first took over here," said Anne, still clutching the mop tightly.

Was this a breakthrough? Adam smiled nervously and told himself it was a breakthrough.

"Did - um - did I?"

"I remember it," said Anne, with a slight emphasis on the I.

"Ah yes," said Adam, telling himself firmly that it was impossible to murder someone with a dishmop. "So I did. Well, it's really not improved, has it?"

"I wonder," said Anne, calm and terrifying, "what it is that you'd like me to do?"

"Well, I'd like you to get it repaired, of course," said Adam, feeling as if the conversation was finally going in the right direction.

"You'd like me to get it repaired," Anne repeated.

"I think so, yes."

"And how much money were you thinking of putting into the repair?"

He hadn't been looking forward to this question, but of course he'd known it was coming.

"I think I've made my position clear," he said. "There isn't any extra money to put into the circus right now." He wasn't keen on the way her fingers were tightening around the dishmop. "So we're looking for maybe people to do a bit of extra work on it in their spare time."

"I have a son," said Anne.

"Yes, I realise that."

"I'm raising him on my own," she went on.

"Yes, I do appreciate it's difficult for you -"

"On a salary that hasn't gone up for the last three years," she said. "That's actually a pay-cut, thanks to inflation."

"It's the same for all of us, you know, including me, in fact I took a ten per cent cut myself last -"

"Every night," she said, "I put my son to bed, and then I open up the carousel, on my own. I keep it open the whole time the circus is open. Every single night."

"Yes, yes," said Adam. "I know you haven't missed a day since I came here, your sickness record's amazing, but -"

"Then when we shut the gates," she continued, "I close up, and then I cash up, and I fill in the records. I record how many riders per run. I calculate average occupancy rates on a fifteen-minute basis, so you can see exactly how the peaks and troughs fall. Once a quarter, I complete the profitability analysis. I calculate fuel costs, and downtime costs, and transport, and depreciation, and I make sure the ride's still in the black. I balance the books every single night, and I'm always ready when Rommel comes by to collect the money. I get to bed about two in the morning. And then my son gets up at seven."

"*Seven?*" said Adam, slightly appalled. Outside of the circus, that was the equivalent of getting up at about half-past three.

"Seven," she said. "Because that's the time little boys *do* get up when they're put to bed at seven thirty every night."

Adam swallowed.

"And then," continued Anne, "when he goes off to see Angela for his lessons -"

(*I will not, not,* not *do anything that shows I don't have the faintest idea who Angela is,* Adam vowed to himself.)

" – then," said Anne, "I get on with running our home. Which, I can assure you, is a full-time job."

Adam glanced around the caravan. Apart from the pots in the sink, it was immaculate. Especially compared to his own caravan, which was cleaned once a week by Niall, and was fairly disgusting in between.

"So," Anne continued, "as you can probably imagine, I don't really have a lot of spare time for coming up with good ideas for how I can get the carousel fixed up with no time and no money and no extra help."

"Er," said Adam tentatively. "Maybe you could…um…spend less time cleaning, just sort of let the housework go a bit? I mean, ha ha, I don't clean every day, and I don't seem to have died of it yet…?"

Anne laid the mop carefully down on the side of the sink and reached for an old-fashioned morocco account book. There was a faint spot of colour in each cheek, and her eyes were very bright.

"But," she said, as if Adam hadn't said a word, "I'd be very happy to let you have a look through the accounts to see if *you* can find a way to do it. Because I'm not nearly as clever as you and I'm sure there'll be lots of great ideas I haven't even thought of because I was too busy washing up frying-pans and folding t-shirts and cleaning floors and wiping down surfaces and scrubbing toilets and putting toys away to have the time or the energy to think of them."

Adam swallowed.

"Sir," she added, as an afterthought.

"Right, then," said Adam. "I'll do that. Nice talking to you. I hope the rest of the…washing-up…um…goes well for you."

He took the book from her hand, and fled.

He hadn't seen Helen's ornate wooden caravan for weeks. He wandered hopefully around the edges of the circus in case it had arrived again, but there was no scent of cookies and vanilla, and no brightly-painted panels, and no friendly arm holding out a mug of tea.

Disconsolately, he returned to his own caravan, noting with displeasure the way the dust hung in the air as the thin sunshine streamed in through the window. He wanted a glass of water, but none of his glasses were clean. He put a kettle on to boil so he could wash one up, then took it off again. Why pick on that one small task when there was so much else to go at?

He sat down at his table with his smeary glass of water, and opened Anne's account book.

An hour later, he was no further forward. The books were perfectly kept – a meticulous angry record of exactly what was happening to the carousel, hour by hour, almost minute by minute. He had never seen so much effort expended on such a basically useless exercise. Who cared if there were ten per cent more riders between 7:45 and 8:00 than there were between 8:00 and 8:15? Were they going to somehow put on more horses at peak times? Take a few off in the quieter moments? What could anyone do differently with such impossibly detailed information?

The woman's insane, he decided. *She's got obsessive-compulsive disorder, she must have. I read about that once, they clean all the time and count things – maybe I can pay her off and get someone more normal in, someone who I can actually work with –*

(*Someone you're not frightened of,* you mean, a small voice said inside his skull.)

"Yes," he said out loud. "I'll pay her off. That's a much better plan. A small lump sum maybe, and she can go off somewhere else and, and, and -"

(*And what?* murmured the voice in his head. *What's an ex-carousel owner supposed to do in the world with a small lump sum and a little boy to look after?*)

"Oh, for God's sake," said Adam crossly, and turned the page. A loose sheet of paper fluttered to the floor, and he bent to pick it up. Then he caught his breath in astonishment.

The white dragon poured across the paper in a flowing elegant sinuous curve, its huge head with its wise golden eyes peering back over its shoulder, blue mane and silver whiskers streaming. Its scarlet mouth sneered in mocking invitation, and its claws were sharp and bright and beautiful. Its pelt was dappled and glossy, like a white horse in the sunlight. It was so vividly alive that it took Adam a good minute to realise that it formed a circle, and its back was articulated, and there were places where the moulding of its back formed seats, and spiralling golden poles pierced its long body.

A minute later Adam was tearing across the circus ground towards Anne's caravan.

"Hello again," said Adam, trying to get his breath.

"Have you finished with my account books, then?" asked Anne, polite and chilling.

"I don't want to talk about the stupid account books," said Adam impatiently. Anne drew in a breath, but he was too excited to notice. "I want to talk to you about this." He waved the sheet of paper he'd found.

Anne's face turned a dull shade of brick red.

"Where did you get that?" she demanded, and for the first time there was a hint of passion in her voice.

"It was in the account book," said Adam. "Did you draw it? It's amazing."

"I apologise," said Anne. "It shouldn't have been in there."

"No, don't apologise," said Adam. "I – I mean, how much would it cost? It looks expensive, but -"

"It is expensive," said Anne. "Too expensive. I thought you'd have known that as soon as you saw it. What with you being so good with numbers and all." She took the paper from his hand.

"So you've had it costed, then?" said Adam. "Maybe we can look at the books, I don't know, work something out - no, no, please – look, I am actually your boss, you know – no, *don't* close the door, I wanted to talk to you -"

The door slammed. Adam banged on it hard.

"Let me in!" he shouted.

Anne opened it again.

"Would you mind awfully," she said, "if you didn't break my door down? Only this caravan is the only home I've got." With exaggerated carefulness, she closed the door again.

"Please let me in!" Adam begged.

The small window over the kitchen opened, and a crumpled piece of paper was tossed out. Adam knew before he picked it up that it was Anne's drawing. The window closed again, and he saw her face, red and furious, peering out at him like an angry demon. Then it disappeared in a fine mist of cleaning-spray and a yellow duster. Anne was washing the windows.

Adam picked up the paper and wandered back across the showground.

When he returned to his caravan, someone had washed out his favourite mug and made a fresh pot of tea. He looked around eagerly, but there was no sign of Helen. However, when he picked up the mug, there was a little note folded up beneath it:

Where there's a will, there's a way.

Adam smoothed out the dragon picture. Even crumpled and muddy, it looked powerful enough to leap off the page.

"She's right," he said out loud. "It would cost a fortune. There isn't enough money."

He stared at the dragon, beautiful and tawdry and crumpled. He could have sworn it winked at him.

After a minute, he reached for Anne's account book, and began to look through it again.

It was after one in the morning when Anne finally opened the door to her caravan to find Adam standing by her sink, doing the washing-up. She put her book down on the table and stared.

"I'm sorry," Adam said before Anne could speak. "I know it's rude to come into someone's home and start cleaning without asking first. But I have to talk to you, and I know you don't have a minute to spare, so I thought I'd better make you some free time. I want to talk to you about building your carousel."

"This isn't funny," said Anne.

"Oh, I'm never funny," said Adam gravely. "I'm not clever enough to make people laugh. I'm not clever enough to do magic tricks either. Or dive off the North Tower. Or ride a horse standing up. Or design the most beautiful carousel ride I've ever seen in any circus, or any fairground, anywhere, ever. But I'll tell you what I am good at, or at least I hope I am. I'm good at finding ways to make things happen. And if I can't find a way to make your dragon carousel happen, then I don't deserve to call myself a circus owner."

"It'll cost too much," said Anne tonelessly. "That's what Mr Santiago said. He said, *It doesn't matter how good it looks, it'll never pay back. There are only so many seats on a carousel ride, and there are only so many times you can run it during one night, and people won't pay more just to sit on a different animal.* He told me to stop dreaming and concentrate on my work." She wiped her nose crossly with the back of her hand. "I don't know why I'm even telling you this."

"Ah, but we're not just going to sell seats on the carousel," said Adam. "And we're not going to build the dragon ride either, not yet."

"Of course you're not," said Anne. "You don't need to tell me that."

"But we will," Adam continued. "We'll need about three years, I think."

"What are you talking about?"

"First," said Adam, "we're going to get someone else to come and run the ride for you in the evenings. The Clowns are over staffed, they never have the whole troupe in the ring every night. I'll transfer one of them over."

Anne snorted.

"Good luck with that," she said, with some feeling.

"I know," said Adam, sighing, "but I've been putting off dealing with them for months, it's about time I got down to it." He shook his head and took a deep breath. "So, someone else takes over the ride."

"And what am I doing while someone else is doing my job?" asked Anne, rather acidly.

"I want you to design things for me," said Adam. "First, I want a new poster. I want the most beautiful poster the circus world has ever seen. I know you can do it," he said as Anne opened her mouth to protest. "While I was waiting, I folded your laundry. Your little boy's t-shirts – they're extraordinary. I can't believe I never noticed them before. Did you do them all yourself?"

Anne blinked.

"And when you've finished the poster," he continued, "we're going to put your poster on t-shirts, and sell them. Adults and children, all different sizes. We'll need to sell a lot of them, but that's all right, because we get a lot of customers. And they're all going to want one, because your poster will be beautiful."

"It might not be beautiful at all," said Anne. "I might draw something awful and terrifying. Just to spite you."

"Then our poster will be awful and terrifying. I'll take the chance. Anyway, I don't want just one."

"Oh, so now I'm drawing *lots* of posters?"

"Four a year. We'll change it every season. If the t-shirts go well, we can print copies of the posters as well. They'll be collector's items."

Anne was staring at the mop in Adam's hand, which was dripping soapy water onto the floor. Adam laid it down hastily on the sink.

"Also," he said, "I'm going to take off one of the horses every week, so you can re-paint them. However you like. I'll leave it up to you. By this time we get to Vaduz, the whole carousel will be refitted. Also, I'd like your advice on the costumes."

"I can't sew!" Anne protested. "And besides, that's Jean-Paul's job, he's always made the costumes, it'll break his heart!"

"You don't have to sew," said Adam. "You just have to have ideas. I wouldn't dream of moving Jean-Paul on. I just want you to advise. That's what artistic directors do."

"Artistic director."

"I think that covers it, yes."

"But -"

"And in three years' time," he said, "when we've sold hundreds of thousands of t-shirts, making about a dollar profit on each one, we'll have enough money behind us for a major new item of capital expenditure. We're going to build the dragon carousel, and it's going to be amazing. And your son can be the first person to ride on it."

"My son," said Anne, "is called Joshua. And in three years' time, he'll be twelve. I imagine he'll be a bit too busy trying to look cool to want to be seen dead on a carousel ride. You really need to get better at learning names."

"I know," said Adam. "Sorry. I am trying."

"You didn't even know I had a son until this morning, did you?"

"I didn't," Adam admitted.

Anne picked up one of the glasses from the drainer and inspected it critically.

"And you're a lousy washer-upper. Those glasses are covered in streaks."

"Oh? – Oh. Yes. Sorry about that."

"And I don't have any proper paints for the horses," she warned. "I'll need to make do with whatever I can scrounge up from around the place. I don't know how good most of it'll be."

"Maybe we can look into buying some more?"

"*Maybe.*" Anne sniffed. "Make up your mind. Can we afford it or can't we?"

"Yes," said Adam, recklessly.

Suddenly, Anne grinned. It was the first natural expression he'd seen on her face.

"Only if I can watch while you talk to the clowns about running the carousel."

"It's a deal," said Adam, and shook her hand.

The Trick Dive

The lights were off and the ring was deserted, but the Parisian rain drummed on the canvas of the Big Top like a thousand hands clapping. Adam stood in the centre of the deserted tent and peered up into the dimness.

"I need some lights," he called hopefully. "Anyone around to put on the lights…?"

The tent remained dim and silent, so he took himself off to the huge bank of switches that ran the Big Top's lights and music. Nothing on the panel made any sense to him, so he took a deep breath and began flicking switches on and off at random.

"For crying out loud," said an annoyed voice from the darkness. A man in blue overalls appeared seemingly from nowhere and slapped Adam's hand away from the deck. "Don't do that, you're messing with my levels."

"I was trying to put the spotlights on," said Adam. "Didn't you hear me yelling?"

"I heard something," said the man, looking thoughtful. "I didn't hear my name, though. So it didn't occur to me that you were talking to me."

"Sorry, Bill, I just wasn't sure who was on duty -"

"You see, if you'd yelled, *Bill, I need some lights*," the man continued, "I might have known what you wanted. But you didn't. So I didn't."

"Sorry about that," said Adam, looking ashamed.

Bill shrugged. "S'okay. Last bloke never even bothered to learn my name, never mind everyone's days off. What can I do you for?"

"I just wanted to have a look around," said Adam.

"Right you are." Bill flicked six switches in rapid succession, and a vast bank of spotlights powered into life with a faint hum. "Make sure you turn them off when you're done. Running these blighters during the day'll kill you on your electricity bill." He pointed. "Those six, in sequence. And don't touch anything else or we'll never be ready for tonight."

"Got it," said Adam. "Thanks."

"No problem." Bill picked up his mug of tea again. "I'm around here most of the time. You need anything, just yell."

Beneath the tall canvas peak of the Big Top, heavy vistas of equipment appeared to float in space. Adam had very little idea of how it was all put together. (Well, being honest, no idea. How did it all stay up? Magic? Magnetism? Sky-hooks?) At each end of the ring, the trapeze artists' towers looked too tall and thin to be stable. Adam wiped his sweaty palms on his trousers and told himself it was fine, no-one was asking him to go up there. About two thirds of the way up the North Tower was the platform used by Marcel, the trick-diver.

Adam looked at it thoughtfully.

"Bill," he called. "Do you know how tall the dive platform is?"

"Twenty-five foot," said Bill from right behind him. Adam jumped. "That's about seven point six metres in new money."

"And the Trapeze tower?"

"Forty foot, twelve point one metres."

"Yes!" said Adam, writing the figures carefully down in his notebook, and grinning from ear to ear. "Thanks."

"That it, then?" Bill seemed disappointed.

"That's it," said Adam, and disappeared. Bill sighed, and turned off the lights.

Hurrying back to his caravan, Adam was delighted to see the old wooden caravan back in its usual place. He ran eagerly up the steps and knocked on the door.

"You look pleased with yourself," Helen observed. "Here, have some tea."

"Where have you been?" demanded Adam, taking the green mug and inhaling the fragrant steam. "I haven't seen you for ages."

"That's because you don't need me as much as you used to. Besides, I do have other people to take care of as well, you know."

"Other circuses?" Adam was surprised by how jealous he felt.

"All sorts of businesses," she said, smiling mysteriously. "This only looks like a caravan to you because you're a circus owner."

"So what would it look like if I was running a greengrocers?" asked Adam.

"If you ever open a greengrocers, you'll find out. Why don't you tell me what you're so pleased about?"

"I've got an idea," said Adam, opening his notebook.

"That's a good place to start. What's your idea? I like the posters you've got Anne working on, by the way, that was excellent thinking."

"Thanks," said Adam, pleased. "Well, I think this one's even better. You see, Marcel only dives from twenty-five feet up."

Helen looked amused. "That's quite a long way, you know."

"Well, yes I *know*, but it's not the highest that anyone's ever done it," said Adam. "But I was reading this thing last night, and apparently there's a new technique you can use that lets you dive from much higher. How much cooler would it be if he dived from the top of the Trapeze tower instead?"

"Mmm. And how much *higher* would it be if he dived from the top of the Trapeze tower instead?"

"Another fifteen feet, but -"

"Is that even possible?"

"Oh yes," said Adam. "There's this calculation. It works out the ratio of height to weight to water depth. And there's this new technique you have to learn – you sort of spread yourself out -"

"Who sort of spreads himself out?"

"Well, Marcel, of course," said Adam crossly.

"And he's happy with this, is he?"

"If he dives from the top of the Trapeze tower he'll break the world record," said Adam. "I just need to find out how much he weighs so I can check the numbers."

"You're going to start this conversation by asking him how much he weighs?"

"I'll see you later," said Adam, and bounded out of the caravan.

"Hi," said Adam. "Marcel, isn't it? Marcel. How are you doing? I wanted to ask you something."

Marcel was small and slight and Gallic-looking. He looked at Adam warily.

"I wasn't expecting visitors," he said. "I have a mess."

"Oh, that's all right," said Adam. "My place is just as bad, I'm sure. Could I just come in for a minute? There's something I want to talk to you about."

Sitting at the tiny table by the window, Adam spread out his treasures. A copy of *The Physics of Shallow Diving*. A series of scribbled calculations. A sketch of a flier headed, SEE MARCEL DUCHAMPS TAKE THE HIGHEST SHALLOW DIVE IN THE WORLD!!!

Marcel studied the details of the flier.

"You require me to dive off the top platform?" he said at last.

"World record," said Adam. "We'll get in touch with the Guinness people and everything. You'll be world famous! Our new star act."

"I don't understand," said Marcel.

"It's all right," said Adam. "It's scientifically proven. All I need is your weight so I can check the calculations, but, well, look at you – not a pick on you, is there? You can't weigh more than about ten stone soaking wet."

"Fifteen feet higher," said Marcel, wonderingly.

"World record holder," said Adam, trying to sound encouraging.

"Forty feet!"

"World record!"

"During which I could die!"

"It's scientifically proven that you won't!"

Marcel and Adam stared at each other. Adam suspected they were not speaking exactly the same language.

"I am required to dive from twenty-five feet," said Marcel, sounding desperate. "I will not dive from forty feet, I absolutely will not. Do you hear me? It is too high."

"The trapeze artists do it."

"I am not a trapeze artist, I am a trick-diver, and I don't care to be the Guinness World Record Holder!"

"But then you'd be the very best in the world," said Adam. "Don't you like the thought of being the very best trick-diver in the world?"

For a moment he thought he had him, but then Marcel shook his head stubbornly. "No. Not if I am required to jump to my death."

"You won't die," said Adam. "It's not just me saying it, it's been properly calculated. Some bloke spent years of his life working this out."

"Then why do not you get *him* to come and dive into twenty-four inches of water from forty feet in the air?" said Marcel, looking mutinous.

"Look, you already dive from twenty-five feet! What's the big deal about going just a little bit higher?"

"Just a little bit higher?" Marcel was pale with disbelief. "Just a little bit higher? Have you *ever* been up there, you yourself? Have you tried to aim to a tiny little target in the precise position to not break your neck? Well, have you?"

Adam and Marcel studied each other carefully.

"Come with me," said Marcel suddenly. "We will go to the Big Top and go up the tower and I will show to you what I mean."

"No, it's all right," said Adam. "Forget it."

"No," said Marcel. "Really. I wish you to know that I am not being difficult or horrible. It is just not possible."

Skinny and determined, he marched Adam into the Big Top and to the base of the tower.

"Come up to my platform," said Marcel, skipping lightly up the ladder.

"No, really," said Adam. "It's fine, you're right, it's too high, I get it -"

"You see, the trapeze artists, they have the net," said Marcel climbing past his own platform and up to the top of the tower. "So although they *look* as if they work at the bigger height, their maximum potential fall is ten feet only. If you come up, you will see."

"I can see just fine from down here, thank you."

"No, please – you must come and see. It is important to me. I do not wish to be difficult, you are a good ring-master, your changes are good, but I need to show to you -"

"I can't go up there!" Adam screamed. "I'm afraid of heights!"

There was a long silence. Adam couldn't see Marcel's expression, but he sensed Marcel was trying very hard not to make the obvious retort, i.e. that a man with a chronic inability to climb a stepladder was in no position to criticise another man for refusing to dive off a forty-foot tower into a pool of water.

"I'm sorry," said Adam at last, as Marcel climbed quietly back down the ladder. "You're right. I'm not being fair. You are only contracted to dive from twenty-five feet up."

"Thank you," said Marcel, with dignity.

"The thing is," said Adam, "To me, all heights are the same, because they're all scary. So I thought maybe they'd look that way to you as well. All the same."

"Really? Well, please believe that there is a big difference."

"I suppose I was just hoping you might feel like trying something new."

"It is too high," said Marcel.

"I know," said Adam wretchedly, and wandered back to his own caravan.

"Bill?" Adam peered into disorganised tangle of cables, boxes, poles and mysterious…stuff…that lurked behind the canvas panel. Was Bill making a *nest* back here?

"Hey." Bill loomed out of the blackness. "Nice to see you again. I don't get many visitors."

"I wanted to ask a favour," said Adam, swallowing hard. "Is it okay if I – um – if I climb up the North Tower?"

"If you like," said Bill. "I'd best come with you, just in case. You okay with heights and stuff?"

"Um -"

"Here," said Bill, rummaging out a hard hat. "Elf and Safety and all that. And you'll want this belt and all." He waggled the dangling bunch of karabiners in Adam's direction. "Clip onto the safety line as you go."

"Excellent," said Adam, putting on the belt with great care. Maybe karabiners were the answer. He couldn't fall off the ladder if he was clipped onto a rope, could he? He wiped his palms down his trousers.

Thirteen rungs up the ladder, and he knew he couldn't carry on. His head was swimming, his palms were soaked with sweat and he had already used up all of his karabiners.

"I'm sorry," Adam gasped. "I can't do this."

"You all right?" Bill glanced perilously back over his shoulder, and saw Adam's white, clammy face looming below him. "God almighty, mate – get yourself back down that ladder right now."

Adam tried to unpeel his hand from the rung.

"Take it steady," said Bill. "That's it. One foot at a time. Deep breaths. Clips off as you go - blimey, all fifteen of 'em? Well, not to worry. Nearly there now, that's it…"

Adam thought he might faint with the relief of feeling sawdust beneath his feet once more.

"Sorry about that," he gasped, bending over and resting his hands on his knees.

"Don't worry, happens to plenty of people." Bill looked at him curiously. "Didn't you know you're bad with heights?"

"I knew," Adam admitted, from around his knees.

"So why'd you go up there, then?"

"Because I have to," said Adam, straightening up and taking a deep breath. "Right. Let's try again."

A handful of nights later, the Big Top was brimming over for the first time in months, and so was Adam's heart. In the twilight before the gates opened, Anne had come to his caravan with a large flat cardboard folder. "Here," she said crossly. "This is the first draft of the poster. I don't know why I'm even showing you it. It's the first thing I've drawn in years, you can't complain if it's not right, it's your own fault for getting me to do it. If you don't like it, throw it away and we can never mention it again." When he looked at it, he felt as if his whole body had turned into a huge, triumphant grin.

But even the thought of that glorious splash of colour and beauty wasn't enough to stop the sweat in his palms and the thump in his chest as he looked at the spindly height of the North Tower. The clowns were reaching the end of their act. The Trapeze team were gathering behind him. It was nearly time.

"So, boys and girls," called the head of the Clown troupe. "Shall we welcome the Ringmaster back into the ring?" Adam knew without looking that he was brandishing a custard pie. It was the way the Clown act closed every night. The other thing he knew without looking was the gleam of malice in the clown's eyes as he slammed the pie into Adam's face, just a little bit harder than necessary. Around the ring, the children screamed and clapped.

"Or," said the clown, dropping his voice to a stage whisper, "shall we get him to do something really, really *scary*?"

Another huge scream.

"Or," said the clown, ad-libbing, "we could do *both*? Or is that too mean?"

(*If you make me climb this tower with custard pie all over my face*, Adam thought, *I swear I will – I will -*)

"You still all right for this, boss?" murmured Gabriel, the trapeze team's burly catcher, right by his ear.

"I'm fine," said Adam grimly.

"Can I have the Ringmaster, please!" yelled the clown. "And can I have Gabriel from the Trapeze team! And now, boys and girls…how would you like to see our Ringmaster try out the Trapeze!"

If Adam had been less terrified, he might have enjoyed the yell that went up from the delighted, disbelieving audience.

I can't do this, he thought in a panic, on every single rung of the North Tower ladder. *I can't do this,* he thought as he passed Marcel's diving platform. *I can't do this, I can't do this, well okay, maybe I can get to the top of the tower, but I can't possibly jump off it, nobody in their right mind would ever jump off here, what am I doing, oh no there's Gabriel, he's ready, I have to jump, no I can't, now I've missed it, okay this time, no I can't, okay I have to, I'm up here now, I'm going to jump in five, four, three, I can't, I can't –*

He jumped.

"Nice job," said Gabriel, patting Adam on the back.

Adam's knees shook and his shirt was dank and reeking with sweat.

"I nearly missed," he said. "I forgot to extend my arms."

"Hey," said Gabriel, laughing. "Any catch we both walk away from is a good one." He rubbed his arms. "Let's not do that every night though, yeah? You're a bit heavier than Jenna."

"Oh, don't worry," said Adam. "I won't be doing that ever again as long as I live. Excuse me, I have to go and introduce the tigers."

When he returned, Marcel was waiting for him. His eyes were very bright.

"You were unable to climb the tower one week ago," he said.

"I know," said Adam.

"So why did you do it?"

"I can't ask you to do something I'm too scared to do myself," said Adam. "Anyway, you're right. Never mind the physics – no-one can dive off that height. It's just too high. It's an insane idea."

"Well," said Marcel, "a man with a fear of heights climbing a forty foot tower and jumping off in the hope that somebody else is going to catch him…that is also quite insane. But you still did it." He shrugged. "Circuses are full of people doing insane things for a living. Tonight my Ringmaster took to the Trapeze. I think perhaps I am not being quite insane enough. I shall read your pamphlet. And we shall see. Perhaps you will soon have a Guinness World Record Holder in your team."

"You don't have to do it, you know," said Adam. "You really don't."

"Ah, but perhaps now I want to," said Marcel.

The Tigers Are Killing Us

There was no getting away from it. The tigers were killing him.

Adam leaned back in his chair and rubbed his eyes. Bern in July was hot and horrible. He was tired and cross from hours of thankless slog through the endless paperwork required to ship a hundred and thirty-one people, fourteen horses, one elephant, an assortment of primates, a tank of sea-lions, twelve truckloads of assorted equipment, dozens of mobile homes and – God help him – eight tigers back and forth across the globe. Every country had different regulations; every country had different things they were worried about. Every customs officer had their own awkward questions ("So, your last stop was Amsterdam…and this is herbage for an *elephant*, you say?").

And then, there were his own people. Every performer had their own phobia about apparently vital equipment that absolutely couldn't go with the rest of the cargo ("I don't care what the regulations say, I'm *not* putting my custom made throwing knives in the cargo hold!" – Ted, the knife-thrower). Everyone had their own inexplicable paranoia about certain destinations and transport routes ("Look, boss, you can't send me through bloody Paris. I joined the

bloody Foreign Legion when I was nineteen, didn't I, and then I got pissed off with it and deserted and the buggers are still after me" – Andrew, from the rigging crew). Everyone had their own brilliant plan to speed up the endless passage through border control ("But it is *not bribery* in this country, they *expect* it!" - Rodrigo, on being caught looking furtive in a corridor while tucking a large wad of local currency into his passport).

But he'd been prepared for all of that. It came with the territory. He'd known from the start that it wouldn't be all top hats and tight trousers and cracking a twelve-foot bullwhip. All jobs came with a certain amount of pain.

Nonetheless, the tigers were killing him.

He looked again at the letter he'd received that morning. It was from an organisation called "The Call of the Wild", but despite the odd name and the dodgy logo (anthropomorphic tigers holding hands with children), the contents weren't at all angry and hysterical. Instead it was a nice, well-argued letter outlining precisely why the group's members were concerned about the welfare of the Starlight's tigers, and suggesting some measures he should put in place to help make them more comfortable in their performing lives.

If they only bloody knew, Adam thought. As far as he was concerned, the tigers were positively pampered. They ate better than he did. Their quarters were cleaned daily, whereas his were either cleaned once a week by Niall or (on the weeks when he was too ashamed of the mess to let Niall in) not at all. They had a regular daily swim in their own private pool. They did half an hour's work a night at the most. Quite often, if one of them sneezed at the wrong time or lay down in a different corner of its cage, they wouldn't even do that, because Dmitri would insist they were sickening for something and shouldn't be asked to perform.

Most of all, the tigers had Dmitri, their own personal fifty-three-year-old body-slave, who spent every minute of his day caring for his tigers, reading about his tigers, talking to his tigers, or talking to other people about caring for, reading about or talking to his tigers.

He'd tried to talk to Dmitri about the costs of the tiger act a few times now. But somehow he always ended up flattened by a steamroller of big-cat facts, and running for his life before he accidentally committed to buy them a much bigger cage, or a personal walker, or their own gigantic arena stocked with live prey so they could practice their hunting skills.

The trouble was Dmitri and his tigers were extraordinarily popular with everyone at the Starlight. Other performers went out of their way to cover for him. They joined in with his ridiculous excuses about why either some, or all, of the tiger act couldn't perform. (The Cossack team were the worst culprits, claiming with poker-straight faces that their horses could "smell the difference" between a sick tiger and a healthy tiger, and would go to pieces if they were asked to walk past a holding cage containing a tiger who was about to be ill.) Adam suspected that some of the team gave Dmitri a share of their already meagre pay-checks to keep the tigers in fresh beef hindquarters. And he didn't even want to think about the time in Minsk when the butcher had refused to deliver unless they paid COD, and Adam had walked around a corner and found Marcus, the magician, coolly butchering a goat which (he claimed) he had "bought off a man in a pub". Adam had scoured the audiences every night for angry -looking farming types, and hadn't drawn an easy breath until they crossed the border into Poland.

And then there was the transport, and the vet bills, and the certification, and the customs import forms, all for the (admittedly quite large) thrill of seeing eight (well, eight on a good night) wild-eyed, glossy-coated predators bound all snarly and stripey across the ring and take their ill-tempered places on their podiums. Despite Dmitri's devotion, Adam suspected the tigers weren't much more than half tame.

They were one of the last circuses in the world to still have tigers, Adam knew. It was a unique selling point. Everyone loved Dmitri; everyone loved the tigers. The big cats represented a last relic of a glorious circus tradition. They were a piece of living history. If he was honest, he was secretly proud to be a part of it.

Nonetheless, there was no getting away from it. The tigers were killing him.

"You're a beautiful girl," Dmitri crooned, staring lovingly into the cage. The tiger ignored him and continued to wash her paws. "Yes, you are. Look at how glossy and shiny your coat is. You're the most beautiful girl in the whole world." Then he glanced guiltily over at her companion. "No, that's not true, is it Bathsheba? You're every bit as beautiful as Judith."

Bathsheba yawned, and rolled on her back.

"Look at you sunbathing! Does that sun feel good on your fur? Are you warm now after your swim? That's good. I don't want you getting a cold...oh, hello Adam! Come and look,

Bathsheba's rolling. They do that when they're feeling really relaxed, you know."

"Do they? That's good."

"It is a good sign, I think, isn't it?" Dmitri looked anxious. "Because you read things sometimes about how animals in captivity, especially intelligent animals like tigers, can get very stressed and unhappy. And sometimes it sends them a bit mad. You know, like those polar bears that sit and bang their heads and rock all day." There was actually a quiver in his voice, Adam realised in amazement. "I'd hate for my girls to feel like that. Trapped and unhappy and bored."

"I'm sure they're all fine," said Adam.

"Do you really think so?"

"Um -" Adam looked at the eight well fed, shining beasts lounging indolently in the sunshine. One was gnawing thoughtfully on the remains of a haunch of meat, crunching the bone between strong white teeth (*must remember to pay the vet's bill or he won't sign the shipping certificate*). Two more lay with their heads on each other's flanks, their tips of their tails twitching (*do tigers dream? I wonder what they're dreaming about?*). Bathsheba had finished rolling and was now on her feet, patting at a large red plastic ball that Adam was sure belonged to the clowns (*even the clowns like the tigers, for God's sake...there's no way I can get rid of them*). "Yes, I really, really think so."

"That's good, that's good." Dmitri looked nervous, which usually meant he was going to ask for something. "I'm really glad you came by, actually. There's something I wanted to talk to you about."

Adam was instantly on the defensive, his spine stiffening, his shoulders tensing, his head filling up with a dozen ingenious ways of saying *no*. He was so busy rehearsing his answers in his head that it was only when Dmitri stopped talking and looked at Adam expectantly that he realised he hadn't listened to a word Dmitri had said.

"Er," said Adam, flapping around for clues. Then he saw that Dmitri was holding a letter that looked vaguely familiar. "Oh, yes. The Call of the Wild people? They wrote to me too."

"So you agree?" said Dmitri.

"Well, I'm not quite sure I'd go that far -"

"It's all about the enrichment, you see," said Dmitri. "I think they've got a point. The tigers need more stimulation."

"Look," said Adam. "You know what our financial situation's like. We're still not really in a position to -"

"I was wondering if maybe they could have the run of the Big Top for a couple of hours every day," said Dmitri.

"Sorry, what?"

"Well, we're paying to set it up anyway, so there's no extra overhead at all. And it's got lots of good stuff in there for them, hasn't it? They'd enjoy it, I think. A chance to explore somewhere new, sort of thing."

"It's a big round empty tent! What's to explore?"

"They could have a nice climb all over the seats," said Dmitri.

"How about a nice chew on the wiring?"

"Oh yes." Dmitri looked dashed, then brightened up again. "Well, maybe we could repurpose the performance cages to fence those areas off so they can't get in there?"

"Dmitri," said Adam gently, "you do know the Big Top is made of canvas, don't you?"

"Yes, but maybe we could cat-proof it somehow -"

"I think it's a lovely idea, I really do," said Adam, hoping he wasn't going straight to Hell for telling such outrageous lies. "But I honestly think the only way to tiger-proof a canvas tent is to not put tigers in it in the first place."

"But there has to be an answer," Dmitri said. "There has to be! We're all meant to be doing things differently now, aren't we? Looking for *new ideas*?"

"Well, when I said new ideas I was actually thinking more about how we could liven up our acts rather than -"

"I'm just worried about what's going to happen to them, you see," said Dmitri. "There aren't many performing tigers left any more." He blinked fondly at Judith, who had finished washing her paws and had started on Bathsheba's head. Bathsheba sat patiently as Judith held her still with one massive paw and licked her fur up the wrong way. "They're a dying tradition. Almost the last of their kind. And if I don't look after them properly – if I don't keep them right up to the mark – well, you know what happened when we came through Dublin airport that time…"

There had been placards, and protesters, and an admission certificate that nearly wasn't admissible. Adam winced at the memory.

"I couldn't stand to lose my tigers, you see," said Dmitri.

And the trouble was, Adam thought, no-one else wanted to see them go either.

When he got back to his caravan, he found Helen had let herself in and made a pot of tea and huge crusty doorstep sandwiches.

"I thought you might need me," she said, before he could say anything.

"Well, since you mention it..." (Was he okay about her just letting herself into his private caravan? Yes, apparently he was. Especially when she made him tea and sandwiches.) "Sorry about the mess."

"Don't be. How's the sandwich?"

Adam bit through the thick golden crust into a savoury slab of ham and sweet tomato, and closed his eyes in bliss.

"Fabulous. Especially the bread. Is it some sort of special recipe?"

Helen winked.

"It's Tiger loaf."

"Oh," said Adam sadly, and put the sandwich down. "So you've heard."

"Heard what?"

"There's this new organisation on the scene. Call of the Wild, they're called. Some sort of tiger welfare organisation. Another one. They've written to me and Dmitri telling us about all the new things we ought to be doing to make sure the tigers live happy, enriched lives. And now Dmitri's panicking. Again." He looked at her over the top of his mug. "Ask me what Dmitri's great idea is to help enrich the tigers."

"Let's hear it."

"He wants to give them the run of the Big Top every morning." Helen put her mug down hastily and started to laugh. "The only problem he can see is that they might chew on the wires, but don't worry, he's got the answer to that; he's going to put up their caging panels round the wiring and keep them out that way."

"And how's he going to keep them in the tent, I wonder?"

"Oh, we're still working on that one. I expect he's going to come and see me tomorrow with some plans for gigantic steel panels that'll cost a fortune, weigh about six tonnes and have to be shipped everywhere we go."

"I've got an idea," said Dmitri, tapping on Adam's caravan door.

"I thought you might," said Adam gloomily. "Come on in, why don't you?"

Dmitri sat down in the chair opposite Adam and leaned his skinny brown arms on the table.

"I know it'll cost some money," he said, "but I think it'll really help the girls. And I've looked at lots of ways to keep the costs as low as they can be." Rummaging in his pocket, he produced a scruffy sheet of folded paper and held it out to Adam. Adam unfolded it gingerly, and stared at it in silence.

"I talked to Andrew," said Dmitri. "He said he thought there'd be room for them all in the truck if we shuffle everything round a bit. So we don't need any extra transport."

But it'll still cost us a fortune extra in fuel, thought Adam wearily.

"And we won't need any extra riggers to help put it up," Dmitri continued. "Rommel and Mick reckon they'll be able to lift them between them. And I'll help too, of course," he added.

The more weight we put on the trucks, the more diesel we burn through. We're already on the bones of our arses, we just can't absorb a penny more in overheads.

"And I've checked with Bill and he's sure we can re-use the caging panels to protect the wiring."

And let's not even think about the capital cost of all this steelwork –

"Of course," said Dmitri, "I know there'll be the capital cost. For the steelwork, I mean. And the fabrication. But where there's a will, there's a way, right?"

"Dmitri," said Adam.

"I mean, it's traditional, isn't it? You can't have a circus without tigers, can you?"

"Look," said Adam.

"We can be pioneers," said Dmitri. "We'll show the world that we can keep tigers in the circus, and still keep welfare standards high. They'll be the best cared for tigers anywhere in the entertainment world. Even Siegfried and Roy will come to us for advice -"

"You see," said Adam.

"I just want my girls to be happy," said Dmitri. "They're the only family I've got, you see."

Are you even aware that your "family" would eat you in about half a second if you were available and they were hungry?

"I don't think we can -"

"I couldn't stand it if I thought they weren't happy," Dmitri repeated. "I mean, what would be the point of any of it if I was just making them unhappy?"

We really, truly, honestly can't afford this. There's just no way -

"I'll have a think about it," said Adam, desperately wanting this conversation to be over.

"Thank you." Dmitri's smile was like a gleam of watery sunshine.

"Why did I say that?" Adam demanded, storming into Helen's caravan. "Why did I tell him I'd think about it?"

"It's always lovely to see you, but I'm a fortune-teller, not a mind-reader. Why did you tell who you'd think about what?"

"He did it, you know." Adam tossed Dmitri's sketch onto her table. "Exactly what I said he'd do. He's gone and had plans drawn up for these massive steel screens. And he's spoken to loads of people about it and they're all bending over backwards to accommodate him, but that doesn't change the fact that we just – can't – afford it!"

"But you told him you'd think about it."

"Yes, of course I did. I should have just told him, but I couldn't. Why am I such a coward? I used to be tougher than this, I'm sure I did."

"You told him you'd think about it because you know it would break his heart to hear you say *no*," said Helen. "That's emotional intelligence, not cowardice. Dmitri's an important part of the team."

"That's nice of you, but emotional intelligence isn't going to pay for the tigers' enrichment programme." Adam sat down heavily in her chair. "He's right, they do need more stimulation. It's not fair to keep eight massive carnivores in such a small cage. We're barely squeaking through animal welfare regs as it is. But we're already over-investing! If it was anyone else's business I'd tell them to get rid and have done."

"So, what would you say to anyone who told you to do exactly that?"

"I'd tell them I can't," said Adam. "If I get rid of the tigers, I'd have to get rid of Dmitri too. And that would break everyone else's hearts. Everyone loves Dmitri. Damn it, even I like Dmitri." He shook his head. "He was here when I first came to the Starlight, you know. I remember sitting in a ringside seat and watching while he made his tigers sit in their places and jump through their hoops and roll over and show him their bellies..."

"I remember," said Helen, smiling to herself.

"So what's the right thing to do? Do I get rid of Dmitri and the tigers and tear the heart out of the entire circus? Or do I just stand by and let us bleed to death because they're costing us more than we can afford, and pray that, pray that, oh, I don't know, pray they all die of old age or something before we go bankrupt?"

"You know," said Helen, "Dmitri really does love those tigers."

"I had noticed."

"And everyone else really loves Dmitri."

"Yes, I'd noticed that too."

"I've seen him sit for hours and talk about those tigers. Hour after hour after hour. To anyone who'll listen."

"Is this supposed to be helping?"

"I sometimes think," said Helen, "he enjoys that even more than he enjoys getting in the ring with them."

Adam slumped down in his chair.

"So," said Helen. "Where do you think Dmitri could find a job like that?"

Dmitri's farewell party was a bittersweet occasion, but the sweet far outweighed the bitter. For every maudlin couple leaning on each other's shoulders and declaring it to be the end of an era, there were others clapping Dmitri on the back and excitedly demanding more details about his and his tigers' great move to the new Safari Park.

"You will receive a cottage?" Marcel demanded.

"They'll have twenty acres," said Dmitri blissfully. "And their own pool, specially dug for them. Imagine!"

"Yes, but you will receive a cottage?"

"And I'll be doing talks every day, twice a day. I might even be on the recording. Can you imagine that! An actual recording of me, talking about the girls, for people to play in their cars…"

"But *you* will not be sleeping in a car, will you? You have accommodation?"

"Oh, yes, I get this little place on the estate somewhere." Dmitri smiled happily. "They'll get more variety in their diet, as well. They have deer on the park, you know, and when they need to cull the herd they -"

"My God, they don't let the *tigers* do the cull, do they?" asked Marcus in alarm.

"Oh, no, they send some man out with a gun, I think. But they feed some of the meat to the carnivores afterwards." Dmitri clapped Marcus on the back. "You know, I'll never forget that goat you shot for me that time in -"

"Have another drink," said Marcus hastily. "Tell me again how big their paddock will be?"

"They're all happy," said Adam, astonished. "I'm the man who got rid of the tigers from the Starlight Circus and retired Dmitri, and they're all happy."

"That's because you found the right way to do it. Every business has to let go of the past sometimes. It's how you go about it that counts."

"We might actually stay solvent now," said Adam.

"And more importantly, your team's thrilled about it. And everyone will keep working on their new acts, and the Starlight will keep getting better, and within six months there'll be so much going on that no-one will have time to miss the tigers."

"Did you see that in your crystal ball?" asked Adam.

"When you know people, you don't need a crystal ball," Helen told him.

The Odd Couple

"I'm sick of this!"

"You're sick of this? *You're* sick of this?" A disbelieving snort, audible to Adam right through the wall of the caravan as he stood outside, hand raised to knock on the door. "I can't believe the look on your face -"

"The look on *my* face? You should see how *you* look right now -"

"Oh, so now you want to make this all about me?"

"Don't try and pretend that's not what you want -"

Adam sighed, and turned away. He'd promised Helen that he'd sort out the problems between the knife-throwers, but he could see already that tonight wasn't the moment. And naturally, when he did finally manage to catch them *not* having a row, he wouldn't mention what he'd overheard. Instead he'd pretend that the only problems he'd seen were the glares and the hisses and the muttered remarks that punctuated their (admittedly pretty good) ringside act.

He wasn't the only one to notice their post show rows, as regular and predictable as the world's most horrible alarm-clock, but of course no-one else had mentioned it either. In the circus, where all the walls were made of canvas and foam-filled plywood, privacy was more a matter of polite convention than a reality. Everyone knew everyone else's business – who was friends with whom, who'd smuggled an audience member into their caravan for an illicit tryst, who watched terrible talent shows even though they swore up and down they thought they were trash – but, by unspoken agreement, you kept what you heard in a separate compartment in your head, and pretended you hadn't noticed it at all. Without these Chinese walls, life in the circus would rapidly become unbearable.

He had to pretend not to notice, Adam told himself firmly. It was just the rules. The fact that he hated the very thought of having to talk to them about their relationship was entirely beside the point. It was a matter of professional etiquette. He would come back later.

Except that he'd already been to their caravan nine times, and every time he'd been there they were in the throes of another argument…he'd vowed to himself that they weren't leaving San Marino with this hanging over them…

Next time, he told himself, in the teeth of the evidence. *Next time it'll be different.*

Adam had learned while doing his MBA that the definition of insanity is doing the same thing over and over and expecting the result to be different. Fortunately, before he had to realise he would have to find a different approach from *turning up at their caravan at the time they always had a row,* the knife-thrower came to him. Ted had a firm handshake (which he deployed even though he and Adam had known each other for over a year now) and he got straight down to business, which Adam approved of.

"I've come to ask for your support for a new project," said Ted, leaning across the table and looking Adam square in the eye.

Hoorah! thought Adam. *A fellow businessman.*

"I've been watching the changes you've made to the other acts," Ted continued, "and I've noticed they're all getting more spectacular. Which I think is great, by the way. We need to move forward if we're going to stay competitive. So I've been putting some thought into how I can, well, *sharpen up my act,* ha ha -"

"Ha ha," agreed Adam, thinking what a pleasure it was to talk to someone so clearly on his wavelength. *Wouldn't life be easier,* he mused, *if everyone was as business-like as this?*

"And I've got an idea to run by you."

"Brilliant," said Adam in delight. "Let's hear it."

"Okay, so what we've got at the moment are four basic elements," said Ted.

Adam reached for his pen and began to scribble notes.

"There's the standard profile-throw from a relatively short distance, just to warm the audience up. Well, everyone does that of course, but you have to have it to make the other elements look more complicated. Then there's the trick-shots – you know, the apple on the head and so on. Then there's the two big set-pieces. The turntable throw - harder, but also standard. And finally, there's the blindfold throw. That's the hardest one of the lot. But it's also standard. And I really want our act to be more than standard."

"I see," said Adam, feeling little champagne bubbles of happiness fizzing in his stomach. This was what he'd dreamed about all his life; a circus where the performers wanted - no, *needed* - to be the best, a group of performers who pushed themselves to the limits for the sheer joy of showmanship... *did I really make this happen*, he thought wonderingly to himself, *just by taking a bit of an interest in what they all wanted to do and making a fool of myself a few times?*

"But what I haven't seen anyone do," said Ted, "is throw burning blades while blindfolded."

"Wow." Adam laid down his pen carefully on top of his notebook. "You – um - you want to throw *burning* knives, with a blindfold on?"

"Not knives," said Ted. "*Sai* blades. Important difference."

Adam thought of the triple-pronged Japanese *Sai* glinting in the spotlights, and swallowed.

"Um – is that even possible?"

"Definitely possible," said Ted, with a firm nod. "Difficult, but possible. Definitely. I'm positive. Hundred per cent." He pushed a neatly-typed report across the desk. "I've done some background info for you but you don't have to read it if you're busy."

"But – but won't that be quite, um, dangerous?"

"Only if I mess up. And I won't. Besides, won't it look incredible? *Wouldn't* it, I mean," he added hastily. "Sorry, I'm just excited, I know you haven't said you'll support me yet -"

"Oh, no," said Adam. "I mean, sorry, *no* – I don't mean *no*, I mean *yes*. Yes! Let's do it! Let's make it happen. I think it's a fantastic idea!"

Ted and Adam grinned at each other like schoolboys.

"So," said Adam, forcing himself to remain seated although he really wanted to leap out of his chair and dance for joy. "How do we make this happen? What do you need me to do?"

"Well, there's just one problem," said Ted gloomily. "It's my partner Lola. She won't do it. She says it's too dangerous."

I'll go and see Lola first thing tomorrow, Adam vowed to himself as he carefully hung his Ringmaster's jacket on its padded hanger. Apart from his promise to talk to Lola about all the reasons why she had to agree to Ted's amazing new act, the animosity between the pair of them during the act was becoming downright disturbing. Tonight, Lola had visibly flinched when the three-pronged *Sai* thudded into the board beside her right ear; and when Ted audibly hissed, "Keep still, you stupid bint!" she'd spent the rest of the act struggling not to cry. Their argument that night had begun even before they got back to their caravan, and Adam had noticed Anne and Marcel – in a clear breach of the circus privacy code lurking quietly in the shadows beside their van, keeping a watchful ear out in case things turned nasty. It was long past time to deal with this.

He reached for his alarm clock and set the alarm for 10:30am. After months of painful experiment, he had finally accepted that there was no possible point expecting anything to happen before at least eleven o'clock in the morning, and that plenty of his performers wouldn't even be awake before what they referred to as "the crack of noon".

First thing tomorrow, he repeated to himself, and turned over to go to sleep.

When he awoke the next morning, an envelope had been pushed under the door during the night. The envelope was apple-green, pretty and delicate, and the notepaper inside was a paler tint of the same colour. The note was written in violet ink, which contrasted fetchingly with the paper.

Dear Adam,

I hope you're well and happily settled in to life at the Starlight Circus. It's a pleasure to be part of the team now – the changes you've made have been really positive and I think everyone's much happier.

I wondered if it would be possible to book some time with you at some point in the next week or so? I realise you're very busy and I promise I won't take up more than an hour.

I'm available any time after noon on any day when you have a slot. I don't know if it's easier for you to come to my caravan or for me to come to yours? – let me know what suits you.

With many thanks in advance,

Best regards,

Lola (the knife-thrower's assistant)

Adam stared at the note in perplexity. It was a strangely lovely thing to receive. It was also the oddest, least business-like communication he'd ever received from an employee in his life. It was more like an invitation to a party than a request for a meeting.

And how was he supposed to reply? Was he supposed to write back? And would she consider it rude if he wrote his reply with a biro on ordinary white printer-paper?

I'll just go round to her caravan and see if she's free right now, Adam thought. *Less messing around...*he looked again at the note. It was almost heartbreakingly polite; every line of it oozed the desire to show respect and good manners. Barging in unexpectedly on the sender and demanding immediate action would be as crass as slapping a butterfly.

He reached for a sheet of printer-paper, and scrabbled madly through the clutter on his desk until he found a biro.

Dear Lola,

Thanks for your note. I'm free this afternoon, so let's meet at half two today. I'll come to you.

Best regards,

Adam

Lola opened the door to her caravan before he could knock on it.

"Come in," she said, anxiously ushering him up the steps. "Thank you so much for agreeing to see me. I realise your time's precious."

Am I really that inaccessible? Adam wondered to himself. He'd thought he was doing rather a good job with his open-door policy. Ted had certainly not found it a problem to just charge cheerfully in. The enticing scent of warm vanilla wound around his nostrils.

"I made some cookies," said Lola, busily pouring tea into pretty china cups. "Please have some, or I'll eat them and get fat and won't fit into my costume any more." She laughed, but her expression was vulnerable.

"These are delicious," mumbled Adam, who hadn't had any lunch. "Um – you said you wanted to see me about something?"

"Oh yes," said Lola. "I'm sorry, I don't mean to waste your time. Would you like another cookie? No really, have another one." She handed Adam his cup. To Adam's astonishment, it came with a matching saucer. He tried to remember the last time he'd drunk tea out of a cup with a saucer, and dredged up a dusty memory of being dragged to a Church Fete when he was about fifteen ("It's important to give something back to the community" - his mother, stern in her beige anorak). He'd put his hood up and refused to make eye contact with anyone.

"These really are fantastic cookies," Adam told Lola. Lola blushed.

"So are you happy with how everything's going?" she asked. "I love the new poster. And those t-shirts you had printed! Anne's so clever, isn't she?"

"Isn't she, though?" said Adam, momentarily distracted. "We sold out the first run in two nights. Had to get some more in as a rush-job."

"It's lovely to see her happy," said Lola reflectively. "It was terrible for her when her husband was killed."

"Is that what happened?" asked Adam. "My God, I never realised...I'd always thought -"

"Yes?"

"Nothing. How did he, um, die?"

"He was a Wall of Death rider," said Lola. "One night his motorbike engine blew up when he was right at the top of the wall. It was a bad fall and the bike landed on top of him. Anne was heartbroken. She was just expecting their little boy."

"Have you been with the Starlight that long, then?" asked Adam, somewhat surprised. Lola looked twenty at the most.

"Oh, no. I just got talking to Anne one night and she told me about it." She reached for the teapot. "Let me give you some more tea. And have another cookie. No, really, do. They're best when they're fresh."

Adam wrestled with his conscience for a minute, then gave in and took another cookie. He was surprised to find that he was enjoying himself. But he really did have other things to be getting on with, and this was supposed to be a business meeting...

"So," he said.

Lola smiled at him.

"Um...?" said Adam, trying to sound encouraging.

"Yes?" said Lola, looking at him blankly.

"You said you wanted to talk to me about something?" Adam wondered if he was going mad.

"Oh! I'm sorry, of course..." Lola folded her napkin into a neat diamond shape, and rested her hands on top of it. "It's...it's sort of to do with the act."

"I see," said Adam briskly.

"Well," she said, and hesitated. "Well, it's like this. I don't know if you've ever been on the receiving end of someone throwing knives at you?"

"To be honest, it's never really come up."

"No, I suppose not," said Lola. "Of course, it's not exactly knives any more. We started out with ordinary throwing-blades, but Ted wanted to look flashier, so he switched to *sai*."

Adam was impressed with the venom Lola managed to cram into the word *flashier*, but wondered if they were going to get to the point soon.

"The thing is - it's really quite frightening. I mean, I know that's the whole point of the act – that it looks frightening – but you know – standing there, keeping totally still – it's not easy. And then, when he puts that blindfold on…" Lola continued. "I mean, don't get me wrong, Ted's brilliant. He's absolutely brilliant. He's only ever missed twice." She rolled up the sleeve of her *broderie anglaise* blouse and showed him the wide silvery line of an old scar on her upper arm. "This was when we were learning the turntable act." She pulled up the side of her blouse and revealed another scar just below her ribcage. "And this was when we were learning the blindfold routine."

"I see," said Adam, who didn't see.

Lola's words were tumbling out in a torrent.

"And I've gone along with absolutely everything else he wanted to do," he said, her voice trembling a little. "I learned the blindfold routine, I learned the turntable. I carried on even when he missed – both times. But now – he's got this

new idea for a fire-throw and – and I don't know if I can do it." She was trying hard not to cry, but Adam could see teardrops on her lashes. "There's just so many ways it can go wrong. And if he misses -"

Adam looked at Lola, pale and pretty and defenceless. To his surprise, he felt very protective.

"You see," said Lola, "my whole job is to keep still, keep my eyes open and keep smiling. Even when I'm terrified."

Adam tried to imagine what it would feel like to lean against a scarred wooden board and stay absolutely still while a man wearing a blindfold aimed fiery tridents scant centimetres from your head. He swallowed.

"So," Lola said, discreetly wiping tears off her cheeks. "I was wondering if maybe you could talk to him. He'll listen to you, you see."

"And what is it you want me to say to him?"

"I was hoping you could tell him that you won't authorise the new act...tell him it's too dangerous."

"Hello," said Helen. She was sitting on the steps of her caravan enjoying the breeze that was stirring the hot afternoon air. "How are you? You look worried."

Adam sat down beside her on the step.

"Thank God you're here," he said. "I really need to talk to you."

"Imagine that," said Helen, smiling to herself. "Is this about Ted and Lola by any chance?"

"How do you always – well, yes, actually, it is."

"I take it you talked to them."

"Yes, and now I've made everything ten times worse. They're arguing every night, they both want me to be on their side and I don't have the faintest idea what to do about it. It's a complete disaster."

"A *complete* disaster? With fires and floods and screams and crumbling buildings?"

"Don't tease me," Adam begged. "I'm really not up to it today."

"I'm sorry. What would you rather I do?"

"Tell me what to do. Please."

"Well, I can't promise that, exactly," said Helen. "You know enough now to work out the answers yourself. But why don't you tell me what the problem is?"

Adam frowned.

"Ted wants to do a new act. He's really excited about it. He says it's a world first. Exactly the sort of thing the Starlight needs. The only problem is Lola doesn't want to do it. So I promised Ted I'd talk to her and make her see sense."

"And?"

"And then I went to talk to Lola, and before I could get a word in she was explaining why she doesn't want to. I mean, I'd never really thought about it before, but she's got a point. Those blades are terrifying. Terrifying! Imagine if Ted *did* miss -" Adam shuddered. "She says *she* wants me to talk to Ted and tell him *not* to do it. And I promised I would!"

"Mmm," said Helen.

"So what do I do now? I can't even work out whose side I should be taking. It's like one of those stupid illusions. Is this a white vase, two black heads or one complete idiot?"

"It's a tough one," Helen agreed.

"So which of them is right?"

"Both of them," said Helen briskly, "and also neither of them. They've each got a valid point of view. Your job is to help them reconcile their opinions."

"But they're completely opposing positions," said Adam in despair.

"And that's what makes your job so interesting," said Helen. "Good luck."

"She's got no ambition," said Ted, as he and Adam helped pack up the popcorn stand. "That's the trouble. I've had to push and push for every little change we've made to our act. If it was up to her we'd still be messing around doing County Fairs and village fetes…"

"He's obsessed with success," said Lola, sitting on an upturned bran tub and sewing sequins onto her leotard. "All that matters is him and his career. He never once bothers to ask what *I'd* like. I don't have to stay with his act, you know. I could be a magician's assistant instead, I get offers…"

"So why doesn't she go and *be* a magician's assistant if that's what she really wants?" demanded Ted, hammering in tent-pegs. "I'm not stopping her..."

"He treats me like I'm replaceable," said Lola, polishing the *sai* blades with a soft chamois cloth. "It's awful. I'm a person, not an accessory. He doesn't take any notice of what I need."

"She's always complaining," said Ted, wild-eyed and foolish-haired as he and Adam shared a rare Sunday night beer. "Nag, nag, nag, nag, nag, *you don't do this, you don't do that...* well, why doesn't she *tell* me what she wants rather than expecting me to guess?"

"Do you know," said Lola, putting down her teacup. "In all the years we've been together he's never once made me -"

"Oh dear God," said Adam.

" Made me *a cup of tea*," said Lola reproachfully.

"Why don't you try talking to them both at the same time?" said Helen.

"Because they hate each other," said Adam.

"So?"

"Um," said Adam, sitting on an upturned barrel in the middle of the Big Top.

From their own barrels, Ted and Lola glared at him. If he'd been in the mood to notice, he might have been amused by their identical postures – arms folded, legs tensed, faces set and frowning.

"I thought it was time we talked about things," said Adam tentatively.

"Good, because this whole situation is completely out of hand," said Ted. "We should have started rehearsing the new act already. We've got no chance of being ready for Odessa now."

"We'll be doing that new act over my dead body," said Lola through gritted teeth.

"Is that supposed to be funny?"

"I'm not laughing, am I?"

"Hang on," said Adam; acutely aware that managing tense meetings between workplace couples was not what he was best at. "Maybe we should, um, talk about how we're all feeling?"

"I haven't got time for this," announced Ted, standing up. "I've got work to do."

"What, work like practicing the act, you mean?" demanded Lola.

"Oh, not this again -"

"We hardly ever practice!"

"We practice all the time!"

"Just out of interest, how often do you practice?" Adam asked.

"Three times a week," said Ted and Lola in unison, then looked at each other.

"So," said Adam, into the suddenly charged silence. "That's interesting, isn't it?"

Lola and Ted stared at him in disbelief.

"Do you have any idea," Lola said to the world in general, "how hard it is to stand still and smile while someone *throws knives at you*? Have you got any idea what kind of trust that takes?" she turned to Ted. "You just breeze in like it's all a big game -"

"A big game?" Ted was pale with rage. "A big game? If you had any idea what it takes to actually take out a sharp blade and throw it towards you, knowing that if I mess up I could – I could -"

"Kill me?"

"Stop saying that," Ted screamed. "Stop making horrible passive-aggressive graveyard jokes about how I'm going to hurt you! I need to know you trust me! I can't do the act if I think you're going to flinch!"

"And I can't stand still if I don't trust you to hit your mark!"

"So you don't trust me?"

"Okay," said Adam desperately, "what I'm hearing is that Lola - you're worried about safety and that makes you nervous, and Ted - when Lola gets nervous that makes you worried about her safety? Is that a fair summary?"

"How can I trust you?" Lola demanded, ignoring Adam. "You don't think about my safety, you never have. You're not bothered about me at all, that's why you switched to those *sai* blades without asking me. They scare me to death, those things! You just want your act to be the best in the world -"

"So, Lola," said Adam. "What would you like to get from the act, do you think?"

"Do you honestly think," said Ted, his voice cracking, "that I could throw sharp knives at the woman I love if I *didn't* think I was the best in the world? I switched to *sai* blades because they're safer, you idiot."

"How can they be safer? Those two extra prongs -"

"- are way too short to actually touch you. They're a safety device, you fool. The blade's wider, but the point of contact's absolutely miniscule. So even if I get closer than I should, I won't – you know – I won't -" he swallowed. "I know you're still mad after I missed that second time, every time I see the scar I feel sick -"

Lola was staring at Ted as if he'd just grown a second head.

"But I'm *not* still mad about that," she said. "I'm mad because I thought you didn't care. Why didn't you tell me it was to make the act safer?"

"Why didn't you tell me you were scared of the *sai* blades?"

"This isn't really my forte," observed Adam at last from his barrel, "but does anyone else think we might be having a breakthrough here?"

"We've got an idea for a new routine," said Ted, holding tightly to Lola's hand.

"We thought we'd combine two elements we already have," said Lola.

"The turntable -"

"- and the blindfold."

"Because we know we can do both of those absolutely fine -"

"- and it's just applying skills we've already got -"

"- and it'll look amazing, a world-first -"

" - it'll take a lot of practice -"

"Hang on," said Adam. "Your plan is to throw sharp blades at a moving target, while wearing a blindfold?"

"Yes," said Ted and Lola together.

"And - and you're both happy with that?"

"Yes."

"Well," said Adam, dazedly.

"So," said Ted. "Are you happy for us to go ahead?"

It was on the tip of his tongue to say no, but wasn't this the sort of moment he'd been dreaming of all his life? What was life without a little risk-taking?

"Okay," he heard himself say. "Let's give it a go."

The Accident

It happened in a heartbeat, as these things always do. In that heartbeat, Henry and Belle, the two youngest members of the Trapeze team, looked at each other from their stations on the tops of the two towers, nodded, and leapt. In that heartbeat, everyone had time to see what they were aiming for – Henry catching the trapeze with his arms a fractional moment before Belle caught his feet, a new and dangerous routine with absolutely no room for error, which Gabriel would certainly have forbidden them from attempting.

It happened in a heartbeat, but the heartbeat seemed to last for long minutes, during which Henry made a bad catch and lost his left hand from the bar, and Belle, panicking, tried to catch only his right leg instead of the double-ankle grip they'd rehearsed, and instead of the triumphant finish they'd worked for she pulled him off the bar, and they fell in a clumsy untidy tangle and landed badly in the sagging, ageing safety net, and even though all of this seemed to take forever there was still time before Adam's heart contracted once more for him to hear the scream of horror from the audience and the desperate blare of *Stars and Stripes For Ever* and the tumble of clowns streaming out into the ring, two of them carrying screens to hide Belle and Henry from view, and none of it was quite loud enough to drown out the echo of that faint sickening crack of bones breaking.

"Nothing to worry about, folks!" Adam lied, swallowing hard and plastering a huge grin across his face. "They're trained professionals, they practice falling all the time! Now…" He shaded his eyes with his hand and peered over to where the clowns were grimly building a large inverted pyramid of gigantic baked-bean cans. "*What's* going on over *here?*"

The show went on, as it always had to. The clowns smoothed over the break in the performance with professional ease. Adam submitted meekly to an additional dousing in custard over and above his nightly ration, this time poured from a bucket from halfway up a ladder. Behind the canvas, Bill turned the sound system up several notches to cover the sound of the ambulance's arrival. The lights shone, and the sequins glittered, and everyone smiled a little bit harder than usual to make sure no-one in the audience could possibly guess they were falling apart inside.

But when the lights went off and the gates were locked, and everyone retired to their caravans, Adam lay awake and stared at the ceiling in quiet terror. This was the first accident that had happened on his watch. It had happened because he'd told everyone to push themselves. Belle and Henry had been trying to impress him.

"It was my fault," he said to the ceiling.

"It was my fault," said Gabriel, hollow-eyed and grey-faced. Adam had got up at six o'clock in the morning and gone for a walk, unable to face the silence of his caravan any more, but Gabe looked as if he hadn't even gone to bed. He was pacing back and forth in front of the stables, hunched into a huge battered overcoat. Underneath, he still wore his white lycra costume. "I should have known what they were up to. They're my team, for goodness sakes…"

"I called the hospital," said Adam. "They're going to be all right."

"They're never going to be all right," said Gabe, tearing savagely at his thumbnail. "They fell. They're just kids and they fell."

"It's not your fault," said Adam, flattened with guilt. "It's mine. I encouraged them into it. All that rubbish about getting everyone to stretch themselves -"

"They're not old enough to get over something like that," Gabe continued. "They'll be off their feet for weeks and then they'll get back up there and they'll freeze. I've seen it before and I'm telling you, that's what's going to happen."

"I'm in charge," said Adam. "That makes it my fault, okay?"

"We're going to have to go back to the basic routine for a bit," said Gabe. "I don't think anyone's feeling confident enough to push themselves out of their comfort zones today."

"No, of course," said Adam. "Look, it's really not your fault, you know."

"I deserve shooting for not realising what they were up to," said Gabe, resuming his pacing.

"It is my fault, I think," said Marcel, standing in Adam's doorway. "I'm so very sorry. I should have known."

"How can it be your fault?" Adam demanded incredulously.

"They saw me rehearsing for the new insane dive," Marcel said. "They wanted to know what I was doing. So I told them, *The Starlight is changing, and I do not wish to be left behind. As performers, it's important that we challenge ourselves.*" He struck himself on the forehead, a gesture so Gallic that Adam, if he hadn't been so miserable, would have been tempted to laugh. "What was I thinking? I am so sorry, Adam."

"It's absolutely not your fault," said Adam. "If it's anyone's fault, it's mine. I should have been on top of what was happening. I sort of knew there was something going on, ever since we arrived in Vaduz. I kept coming into the Big Top and feeling like someone had been in there on the trapezes, but I never thought to -"

"Do you think," said Marcel, "that perhaps I make a mistake with the dive? Is this a time to be insane? I think not. I think perhaps I won't be diving from forty feet up after all. Not this time. I'm sorry, but I do not feel -"

"Don't be sorry," said Adam. "I don't blame you."

"It was my fault," said Anne, mending a pair of jeans. "I should have told you what was going on."

"What?" Adam was astonished. "But – but how did *you* know when I didn't?"

"Belle asked me to make her a new costume," said Anne. "She didn't want to go to Jean-Paul." Her fingers whipped the needle in and out, in and out, drawing the frayed edges of the denim together into a neat clean line. It would have been a comforting, cosy sight, except that tears were streaming down Anne's face and it was five o'clock in the morning two days after the accident and neither she nor Adam had slept. "She wanted to keep it a secret. It was supposed to be a surprise." She swiped angrily at her face with the sleeve of her blouse. "I should have known what she was up to. I should have told her not to. You'd think after the things I've seen I'd know better than to -"

"It wasn't your job to stop her," said Adam, trying to pretend he hadn't noticed Anne was crying. He suspected that if he showed the smallest sign of sympathy, she might kill him.

"Of course it was my job to stop her," said Anne. "Whose job is it to look after the kids if it's not the grown-ups?"

"You know, everyone working here mostly thinks the accident was your fault," said the chief clown, catching Adam's eye in the mirror as he painted on a terrifying, accusatory whiteface.

Finally, thought Adam with mordant humour, *finally I found something we agree on.*

"It was my fault," Belle whispered, tears leaking out from behind her eyelids. The hospital bed was short and thin, but she still looked ridiculously young and small. "I jumped too early."

"It was my fault," said Henry, pale and resolute, his leg absurdly huge in a vast white plaster cast. "I mistimed the catch."

"It wasn't either of your faults," Adam told them both. "For God's sake, you're -" he wanted to say, *you're just kids*, but remembered in time how annoying that could be even when it was patently true. "It's *my* fault. I didn't keep a close enough eye on what you were doing. I've been giving everyone too much freedom. I need to tighten up and make sure we don't have a failure like this again. From now on we'll have a rule that no-one introduces anything new into their act without clearing it with me and the head of the act first, that way we won't have any more problems like this one. But it's not your fault, okay?"

The despairing silence from both of them was not reassuring.

"It was my fault," Adam told Helen on Sunday night, after a frantic day of thinking and planning and paperwork. The tea in his mug was fragrant and aromatic, but it did little to console him.

"You seem very sure about that," she said.

"I am very sure about it. I'm in charge. The buck stops with me. When something goes wrong, I take the blame and I make the changes we need to ensure it never happens again.

That's what being in charge means. Is there – is there alcohol in this tea?"

"Brandy. Why is blame so important to you?"

"You've got to blame someone," he said.

"Have you?"

The brandy radiated out from his stomach and warmed his chest. Adam savoured it for a moment, then pushed the mug away from him. *I don't deserve brandy*, he told himself miserably.

"I suppose you're thinking you don't deserve brandy," said Helen, pushing the mug back towards him.

"This isn't funny," said Adam.

"I'm not saying it is funny. It's very, very serious. Probably one of the most serious things that's ever going to happen to you. How you handle this is going to affect everything in the circus for years and years to come."

"I know," said Adam. "I've been thinking about it all day. We need more processes to stop something like this ever happening again." Helen looked dubious, but Adam didn't notice. "We've simply got to eliminate the risk of failure. What I was thinking was, we need at least three levels of sign-off before anyone tries anything new or different. First they'll need to go to the divisional head."

"But you don't have any divisional heads, do you?"

"No, I know, but I'll create them. I was thinking Gabriel for the acrobats and other physical performers, Ted for the illusionists and Scary Doctor Whiteface for the rest. He'll like that."

"You'll never build a good relationship with him if you call him *Scary Doctor Whiteface*, you know. You really ought to call him by his proper name."

"I can't think of him by his proper name, it doesn't suit him. Anyway, the divisional head will do a basic initial review against a pre-agreed checklist of criteria."

"I see," said Helen, pushing the mug of tea another inch in his direction.

"Then," said Adam, absent mindedly taking another mouthful, "assuming it passes the divisional head, I'll want a full safety review. That'll be done by Bill. He'll provide me with a full report to a pre-set template." He squinted suspiciously at the mug. "This is quite strong, isn't it?"

"It's just as strong as it needs to be. How does Bill feel about that?"

"Oh, I haven't asked him yet. But I'm sure he'll be fine with it."

"He's not really much of a one for paperwork, you know."

"I'll get him some training."

"I'm really not sure that's the problem -"

"Then," said Adam very loudly, "we can bring all the remaining new ideas to the monthly committee meeting. I'll have all the senior performers there, and we can invite the idea proposers to come along and share their ideas. We'll use the experience and expertise of everyone to decide if it's safe to proceed to the next stage – anything too dangerous can be rooted out immediately."

"So there's still more to this process?"

"Oh yes, of course. Once we've done all the basic evaluation work, we can look at the risk/reward profile."

"The risk/reward profile."

"Yes. I'm working on a template right now. It's designed to ensure that only the very lowest risk ideas actually get through the screening process. I want to eliminate all risk of failure as far as I possibly can."

"Just out of interest, how are you defining *failure*?"

Adam glowered at her.

"I think two of my youngest performers nearly dying last week qualifies as a pretty damn big failure, don't you?"

"But where do you think the failure actually occurred?" Helen's face was intent. "Was it when they tried something new? Or was it when their new idea didn't work out quite the way they planned?"

"What's the difference?" Adam took another mouthful of tea. "Blimey. This gets stronger the further down the mug I go. The point is, this new process will make everything safer. We'll cut down on risky new ideas and dangerous inventions. The less time people spend doing new things, the less chance we have of something going wrong."

"So once your new…process…kicks in, nobody in the whole of the Starlight Circus will be allowed to try out anything new at all?"

"New ideas," said Adam, "are how accidents happen."

"I see. Would you like another mug of tea?"

"I think I'd better, actually. That brandy's going right to my head. Besides, that's just the beginning."

Helen poured another mugful for him from her spotted teapot, adding a generous dollop from a silver hip-flask.

"No, I really shouldn't…"

"Yes, you really should. So, tell me more about how this is just the beginning."

"Well, once we've got the new ideas process in place, we're going to have to review everything else we do too. I'm going to go through every act in the circus, top to bottom, and get rid of all the dangerous parts."

"Is that actually possible, do you think?"

"Well, it might mean some compromises, but yes, I think it's possible."

"Tell me more."

"Is this stronger than the last one?" Adam took another mouthful of tea and swilled it thoughtfully around his mouth. "Well, the high-wire act, for example. It's too high, I realise that now. We'll have to lower everything by a good ten feet or so. And Ted and Lola, I'm going to talk to them about increasing the throw margin, so Ted's knives are landing much further out from where Lola is on the board. I even thought I might talk to Paolo about building some sort of illusion to replace the actual knife-throwing part…"

"You want a knife-throwing act where no-one throws knives?"

"Well, you have to admit it's a bit of a hazard, isn't it? I can't believe I never realised before just how – how crazy dangerous all the stuff we do here really is. I mean, what are they all thinking? How do we even get away with it? But I'm in charge now, I'll sort it out. No more failures, ever. It's too hideous for everyone." He drained his mug of tea and stood up, slightly unsteadily. "Um. How much brandy was there in that mug of tea?"

"Oh, you know." Helen smiled to herself. "Enough to give you a good night's sleep. Starting round about ten minutes from now."

"The floor's moving. Is the floor moving? I think it's moving." Adam clutched the edge of the table. "I was going to have a meeting."

"Yes, I know. Don't worry, I'll tell everyone you're -"

"Drunk?" Aiming for the doorway, Adam lurched into the wall, making the caravan shake. "Please don't, they'll never respect me again…"

"I was going to say, *thinking it over some more,*" said Helen.

"I don't need to think it over some more. My mind's -" Adam yawned – "my mind's made up. I'm not going to have failure in my circus. Not when it puts people's lives at risk."

"You know, the opposite of *putting people in danger* isn't necessarily *stop people doing anything new or risky.* You might want to think about how you can give them the freedom to fail in a safer environment."

"If you hadn't given me so much brandy to drink I might be able to make sense of that."

"Well, see how it looks in the morning."

"In the morning, Belle and Henry will still be in hospital and I'll still be implementing my new process. Only with a hangover. And in a foul mood." He swayed gently on the caravan steps. "This was really unfair."

"Sometimes I have to take drastic action to stop you doing things you'll regret later."

"I feel sick now." Adam rubbed his stomach. "I'm really cross with you, you know. And I'm still having that meeting. Since you're cancelling it for me, you can tell them all to meet me in the – whoops, who put that rope there – in the Big Top at noon tomorrow."

"Whatever you say," said Helen. "Sweet dreams."

"I'm not sure I'm ever going to sleep again, actually," said Adam, and lurched unsteadily away into the night.

That night, Adam dreamed he was back in his old job. He was working at the drinks company he'd been with for the five years after graduation – something which surprised him even while he dreamed, because surely he'd moved on from this a long time ago? The people in the office seemed unsurprised to see him, though, so perhaps he was meant to be here after all.

He was desperately trying to prepare for a meeting. He had to present to the Board. He had a fantastic new product to show them, which he knew they were going to love. On his desk was a flask of a honey-coloured bubbly drink, cold and sweet and delicious. It was unlike anything else he'd ever tasted, and he knew it was going to be a winner. But he couldn't find the right form to fill in, and without the right form, no-one would listen to his idea.

"Have you filled in the form?" His boss was taller than Adam remembered and was wearing a clown suit. "I need the form filled in."

"It's nearly finished," Adam lied; he hadn't even managed to log onto the network yet. His user-name wasn't recognised, even though he'd used the same one for years and years, *barnumbailey78* and the password, *Starl1ght**. As he stared desperately at the screen, he realised he'd typed his username wrong. He tried again, but his fingers kept hitting the wrong keys.

"We're ready for you now," his clown-boss announced, leading him down the corridor. The corridor was incredibly hot and bright. Glancing down, Adam realised he was wearing a gorilla costume. The costume looked familiar. In fact, it was the one he'd worn on the night he'd first begun to break through to everyone at the Starlight. *The Starlight!* he thought triumphantly. *That's where I'm supposed to be working! Not in this office, filling in forms!*

"No," said the clown, as if reading his thoughts. "You don't work at the Starlight any more. The Starlight closed down because you said it was all too dangerous."

"But -"

"Have you done the form, then? Have you? Because you promised me you'd done the form, remember?"

Adam rummaged desperately in his pockets (he was surprised to find that the gorilla costume actually had pockets) and found a crumpled wedge of folded A4 sheets. He held them up to the clown.

"Are these the right ones?"

"Well," said the clown. "You tell me. Are they the right ones? Because we all know paperwork is what keeps people from making dangerous choices, isn't it?" He pushed Adam in through the door of the boardroom. "In you go."

Inside, the boardroom was crowded with people. Adam's suit was growing hotter and itchier by the minute. But no, it was all going to be all right, he still had the flask in his hand, and once they tasted the drink, everything would be fine.

"I want to talk to you about this new drink," Adam said.

The CEO wasn't listening. She was talking on the phone, and making notes on her notepad.

"Hello?" said Adam. "Can you hear me?"

"Form," said the CEO, holding out her hand without looking at Adam.

"I – look, I haven't got a form, the computer wouldn't turn on. But I want you to try this new -"

"Our process is designed to minimise risk and ensure we avoid failure as much as we possibly can," chanted the head of R&D, with an inane grin. He was wearing one of Anne's t-shirts.

"This won't fail," Adam insisted.

"We can't possibly evaluate that without the right paperwork," said the head of Marketing, resplendent in feathers and purple lycra. "If you're not going to follow proper procedure -"

"Just try it!" Adam screamed, surprising himself. "It's delicious, it'll be a winner! Just bloody try it!"

"There's no need for that kind of language," said the CEO severely, putting down her phone. Her nails were very long and pointed. "I've told you all over and over, there's no room for failure in my organisation. I simply won't have it. These processes are in place to ensure we're totally insulated from the consequences of risky behaviour."

"Just try the drink! Please!"

"We're not interested in *new*. New's dangerous. We're interested in *safe*."

"You have to try this drink right now," Adam insisted.

"Or else what?" asked the head of R&D, grinning and chattering his teeth.

"Or else I'm going to kill you," said Adam, launching himself across the desk. The R&D head fought back, but Adam was too angry to care. He put his hands around the man's throat and began to squeeze, relishing the feeling of his fingers sinking into the man's flesh, deeper, deeper...

He woke up sweating and horrified at himself, to find himself lying on the floor, his duvet wrapped around him like an imprisoning shell. He struggled free and staggered to the tiny kitchenette to splash water on his face.

Where had all of that come from? The real-life CEO of Scotbev had been a brilliant, inspiring woman who had led from the front, walked the talk and drummed into all of her staff the critical principle that none of them could ever afford to stand still. *There are four hundred thousand new people coming into the world every single day,* she'd told them all at one conference. *What makes you think they'll settle for the same old shit we've got now? Never get too comfortable, guys. It's the kiss of death for any business.*

"But then, *she* only made soft drinks," Adam said out loud, pouring a glass of water and gulping it gratefully. "I mean, it's not as if anyone was going to die if she messed up and launched the wrong flavour of soda, was it?"

He remembered again how righteously good it had felt to throttle the head of R&D. The sheer *rage* he'd felt, even in the confines of his dream, at having his idea ignored. *Never get too comfortable*, indeed.

His desk was littered with paper, as it always was. This morning, the dawn light seeped in beneath the blinds and trickled over the careful, meticulous plans he'd drawn up to squeeze out risk from every aspect of circus life; to lower, to diminish, to lock away, to slow down, to take away the sharp edges. *No more failure.* That's what he'd vowed to himself as he stood beneath the harsh lights of the hospital emergency room, praying for the words *they're going to be fine* and all the while convinced he was actually going to hear *let's go into this room so we can talk more privately, I'm afraid I've got some difficult news for you* -

"No more failure," he said into the dimness, to see how it would sound.

No more failure.

"Here's the thing," he said, standing on the bran tub in the centre of the Big Top. If he'd stopped to think about it, he might have taken a moment to congratulate himself on how far he'd come since the last time he'd brought everyone together to talk to them. Then, he'd been wearing a gorilla suit and been half-convinced they would pelt him with rotten fruit rather than listen to him. Now, he had everyone's attention (even the head of the Clown troupe), most people's respect (the Clown troupe being the glaring exception), and Lola had made a mountain of cookies and a gigantic WI-style urn of tea and there was a mug and a cookie for him too.

"Here's the thing," he repeated, praying he was doing the right thing. "What happened last Saturday night was awful. Probably the most awful thing I've ever seen. And I know we all feel responsible."

("I bloody don't," muttered the Chief Clown, somewhere to the left, and just softly enough for Adam to pretend he hadn't heard him.)

"And being honest," said Adam, "the truth is that we probably are all responsible."

There was an incredulous silence. Adam found he was impressed at how much outrage it was possible for a group of people to convey simply by standing still and looking at you *en masse*.

"I don't mean it's anyone's fault," Adam continued hastily, feeling as if he, too, was about to fall from a very high place and land very badly. "I just mean that we all have a share in creating the environment we work in."

His knees were wobbling a little. The bran tub suddenly seemed a very high place to be standing. He stepped off, and instantly felt better.

"You see," he said, "I know Saturday night frightened all of us, and I'm not surprised either. It's a scary, dangerous business we're in. We all take risks, every night of our lives."

("Everyone except you," the Chief Clown murmured with a sickening smile.)

"So my first thought was that we had to make everything safer," he said. "And I know a lot of you had that idea too. Let's stop risk-taking, let's not try new things, let's walk away from the dangerous stuff. Because if we get rid of the risk, then we won't ever have another night when we have to have the music so loud that the audience can't hear -" again he heard the muffled crack of breaking bone, and his throat closed up suddenly and he had to swallow violently several times to force it open again.

"But," he continued, "the thing is…Henry and Belle's act… it nearly worked. It nearly did! It was nearly, *nearly* amazing. They were so close to perfection. And if it *had* come off… we'd all have been throwing them the biggest party of the season."

("If we've got money for a party, we've got money for a salary increase -")

"I don't want to run a circus where no-one takes risks," said Adam, manfully ignoring the voice of doom from his left. "I want to run a circus where we can take risks safely. If we don't fail sometimes, we're getting too comfortable. The problem wasn't that they fell. The problem was that we didn't have a good enough safety net to catch them."

At the back of the crowd, Bill shuffled and glared.

"I don't just mean the actual safety-net," Adam said hastily. "I mean the safety-net where we look after each other. We all sort of knew they were up to something, but we just left them to get on with it. I know a lot of you feel guilty because you didn't stop them…but that's not what we should have been doing. We should feel guilty because they felt they had to hide away what they were working on. We should have been *encouraging* them. We should all have been in here with them, watching and cheering them on and offering suggestions. No-one should ever feel like they have to hide their new stuff away until it's perfect. And no-one should ever, ever have to be afraid of falling."

"Um," said Gabriel.

"Ho," said Marcel.

"Mmm," said Anne.

The Chief Clown's remark was one Adam chose to ignore.

"They're coming out of the hospital this afternoon," said Adam. "And when they come back, I don't want anyone fussing round them and asking them if they're all right and how are they feeling. I want you all to give them a bloody big cheer and tell them they're heroes, and that next time we'll be there to catch them. And Bill, I want a new bigger safety net for the aerial acts, and a deeper tub for Marcel's dive, and let's have a look at those new trick saddles for the Cossack team after all. And I want you all to carry on trying new stuff, but without having to hide, and without having to worry about what happens if it all goes wrong. We can't get rid of failure, not without getting rid of what makes us great. But we can make it less painful when it happens."

The round of applause surprised him so much that he nearly spilt his tea. As he wondered wildly whether he should take a bow, he saw Helen watching him from the doorway.

CHAPTER

Send in the Clowns

Coulrophobia, (n). An abnormal fear of clowns. A term of recent origin (1980s) and not formally recognised in DSM-IV. Nevertheless, many patients (especially children) report an intense dislike of clowns and some experience severe nightmares as a consequence.

This is wasting time, Adam told himself sternly. *Stop messing around and get on with your work.*

'A study conducted by the University of Sheffield found that the children did not like clown décor in the hospital or physicians' office settings. The survey was about children's opinions on décor for an upcoming hospital redesign. Dr Penny Curtis, a researcher, stated "We found that clowns are universally disliked by children. Some found the clown images to be quite frightening and unknowable."'

Adam looked again at his to-do list, just in case something might have magically appeared on it that was both more fun, and more important, than what he was actually supposed to be doing. Slightly disappointingly, this hadn't happened.

The more you put this off, the harder it's going to be, he thought.

'Although clowns are originally comic performers and characterized to humour and entertain people, the image of the evil clown is a development in popular culture in which the playful troupe of the clown is rendered as disturbing through the use of horror elements and dark humour.'

You pay his wages, he reminded himself, and took a deep breath.

He scribbled a terrifying face on the edge of his notebook, and then scribbled it out again.

"Just one minute, please," said the Chief Clown. He sat behind the huge oak desk he insisted on having shipped everywhere the Starlight went, even though it weighed nearly a hundred kilos and took up half the clowns' dressing room. His enormous leather chair (another expensive item on the shipping manifest) made him look like a Bond villain. The clown's back was to the window, and when Adam sat down in his (much less comfortable) chair, the sunlight shone straight into his eyes.

This is almost funny, Adam thought to himself, as the clown made an ostentatious show of tidying away some papers into a drawer and checking his phone for messages. *Almost...*

"So," said Adam, trying to sound friendly. "How are things?"

The Chief Clown favoured him with the kind of dead eyed stare that would have looked at home on a shark.

"Troupe all happy?"

"I'm glad you raised that," said the Chief Clown. "Because as it happens, I wanted to talk to you about what you plan on doing to help improve morale among my team."

Damn it, thought Adam, *he's done it again.*

As far as Adam was concerned, the Clown Troupe remained the one terrible black spot in a circus that was otherwise an increasing pleasure to manage. He was putting all his spare time and energy into trying to improve the relationship – beginning with this weekly update meeting with Scary Doctor Whiteface. (The Chief Clown's real name was Amory James, but Adam found he could only ever think of the man as Scary Doctor Whiteface.) Before every meeting, Adam would carefully agree what they were going to discuss (on the list today was a potential switch in performance running order, options to reduce the troupe's astonishingly high laundry bill, and managing requests for encores). Before every meeting, he would prepare a carefully typed agenda and have it on the Chief Clown's desk by 4pm the day before. ("There's no point sending me anything after 4pm. I'm too busy to look at paperwork while I'm getting everyone ready for a show.")

And, at some inevitable point during every single meeting, Scary Doctor Whiteface would skilfully derail the conversation into a topic of his choosing, then spend the rest

of the meeting berating Adam for all the things he hadn't done but should have done, or shouldn't have done but had done, or should have thought of but hadn't thought of, every remark coming with the clear subtext *you're useless and you know nothing and you're doing a terrible job,* until Adam could bear it no longer and retreated, apologising, from the room.

"What's the problem with morale?" Adam asked. He had once – but only once – made the mistake of pointing out that a particular item raised by Doctor Whiteface wasn't on the agenda. After listening to the ensuing tirade about how solving the important issues mattered much more than petty bureaucracy, Adam had seriously considered whether he was cut out for his job after all.

"You mean you haven't noticed?" Doctor Whiteface raised an eyebrow. Adam cringed. *You're disconnected from your workforce,* the raised eyebrow seemed to say. *You don't even know what your own team are thinking. What kind of a manager are you?*

"Erm," said Adam. Doctor Whiteface sighed. *You're also weak and indecisive,* the sigh told him. "Why don't you fill me in on what you've noticed?"

"Well, they're not happy about the pay situation, obviously," Doctor Whiteface began.

"Yes, and I do appreciate why, but you have to understand we're all in the same -"

"But the thing that's really worrying them," Doctor Whiteface continued, as if Adam hadn't spoken, "are all these demands for them to take on extra workload."

"What? What demands?"

"The demands that you've made," said Doctor Whiteface, with exaggerated patience. *You can't even keep track of what*

*you're doing. Call yourself a manager? No, I have to stop this, why
am I doing this to myself? I know what I'm doing, I'm doing a good
job, I'm sure I am.*

"I don't really know what -"

"Two months ago," said Doctor Whiteface, consulting his
papers, "you demanded that the Clown Troupe take over
the nightly running of the carousel ride. We accommodated
that demand, because we recognise that you'd created
yourself a problem by taking Anne off that ride and giving
her other duties, and you needed us to help you. But surely
you can't be surprised that they're unhappy about the lack
of recognition."

"Ah," said Adam. "But the thing is, you see -" he didn't like
how weak and placating he sounded, and began again. "The
fact is, the troupe's contracted for six nights a week."

"And is there any night of the working week when we don't
perform?"

"No, of course not, but -"

"We fulfil every aspect of our contract to the letter, and
we always have. All we ask in return is that our rights are
respected, and we're not subjected to additional demands
from management which are completely unwarranted."

"There are eight of you," said Adam. "I'm paying eight of
you. And the act only uses six of you every night."

"Well, of course," said Doctor Whiteface, after a tiny pause,
"we're all aware there are some...ambiguities...in the
contract. And we're more than happy to work with you to
iron those out, over time and in an orderly fashion. But what
we're not happy about is for this all to be imposed on us,

from above, without consultation, and without any reference to the impact on everyone's wellbeing."

What have I done that's so terrible? Adam thought desperately. *Am I such a monster? Have I made everyone cross for no reason? I'm paying eight people; I'm using eight people. Is that such an awful thing to do? I thought I was making everyone happier…*

"Of course, as we all know, you didn't grow up in the circus world, so you might not appreciate there's quite a big difference between *performing* and *manning a stall.*"

"But it's still working for the Starlight, their contract specifies working for the Starlight -"

"Of course, you can bring everything down to the minute detail of the contract if you like," said Doctor Whiteface. "But I was under the impression that we were trying to get away from all that sort of petty bureaucracy."

Out of touch, demanding, petty, bureaucratic. Maybe I'll just confess to assassinating President Kennedy while I'm at it.

"The best way to resolve this issue," Doctor Whiteface continued, "would be to implement a pay-rise."

"We can't afford -"

"The alternative," said Doctor Whiteface, "would be to revert to previous working practices until you're in a position to properly reward everyone for their efforts."

"But we can't do that either, I need Anne to be able to focus on -"

"Well, I'll leave that one with you. You can bring me your proposals the next time we meet."

"But all of this was put in place months ago," said Adam. "I don't understand why I'm only hearing about this now?"

"Don't you?"

Because, on top of everything else that's wrong with me, I'm clearly hopelessly out of touch with my own people, thought Adam wretchedly.

He was halfway back to his own caravan before he remembered they hadn't even discussed the laundry bill.

Helen was cleaning the windows of her caravan when Adam knocked on her door.

"Tell me," he begged. "Tell me the truth and I swear I'll listen. Am I a demanding petty bureaucrat who's hopelessly out of touch with his team and never thinks about the human cost of the decisions I make?"

"Where did you hear all of that?"

"Guess."

"Oh, of course, it's Tuesday." She put down her bottle of cleaner and peeled off her bright yellow gloves. "He actually used those words, did he?"

"Yes," said Adam, then paused. "Actually, no. Not exactly. But it's clearly what he meant."

"And do you believe him?"

"No, of course I don't believe him! Well, I don't think I do. No, I definitely don't. I'm not any of those things, am I? I'm not perfect, but I'm doing a decent job. People are happier. The Starlight's a better place than it used to be. It is!"

"There you are, you see? You already know the answer."

"So where am I going wrong?"

"You tell me. Where are you going wrong?"

"I don't know!" Adam shook his head. "You've got to help me. Every time I talk to him it's worse."

"What have you tried so far?"

There was a plate of cookies on the table. Adam sat down and absent-mindedly ate three.

"Formal meetings," he said through a mouthful of crumbs. "Defined agenda, developed by both of us, agreed the day before. Except every single meeting ends up a train wreck. I come out feeling like I've been run over."

"So what else can you think of to try?"

"Maybe we need to get to know each other in a more social setting," said Adam, licking crumbs off his fingers.

"Wonderedifyouwerefreeaftertheshow," Adam blurted out. His palms were sweating with nerves. This was worse than asking a girl out. "Ithoughtwecouldgooutforafewdrinks, gettoknoweachother."

Doctor Whiteface looked surprised, which was possibly the best result he'd had so far.

The night began in a downtown Bratislava bar at eleven sharp. Emboldened by what felt like a blossoming comradeship, Adam opened the thorny subject of shipping costs for Doctor Whiteface's oak desk, and made several joking references to the laundry bill. Doctor Whiteface seemed strangely keen on buying the drinks.

He was unsure of precisely how the evening ended, but he woke up to a chilly grey dawn slumped on the steps of his caravan, fully dressed and with a sense of foreboding.

That night, he was the subject of several shocked looks and Lola burst into tears when he tried to speak to her. After serious interrogation, Marcus finally told Adam that Doctor Whiteface had told everyone that Adam spent the entire evening ranting about the importance of cutting back on useless overheads and a need to become less sentimental, before passing out onto a barmaid and having to be carried home.

"Maybe I need some new techniques for talking to him," said Adam, pale but determined.

"That's certainly worth a try," Helen agreed.

"This proposal about the laundry bill," said Doctor Whiteface, holding it with his fingertips in a way that subtly suggested it was as dirty and unpleasant as the washing under discussion. "There's simply no way we can look at cutting back on washing."

"That's not what I'm saying," said Adam.

"We need clean costumes," Doctor Whiteface continued. "It's unacceptable to ask people to wear clothing spattered with food residue."

"That's not what I'm saying," Adam repeated. "My suggestion is that instead of getting everything dry-cleaned, we look at sending one of the junior team down to the launderette and -"

"I mean, come on," said Doctor Whiteface. "Are we really in such a bad position that we need to be penny pinching off the washing bill? How much management time have you wasted already on talking about this?"

Adam blinked.

"Even without a pay rise," said Doctor Whiteface, "I know my time's worth more per hour than this." He was ostentatiously shuffling a stack of papers as he spoke. As Adam watched, a poster for Bendicks, the Starlight's deadly rivals, rose to the surface. "In fact, some people might think it's worth considerably more."

"If I can't work with him, then I'm going to go around him," said Adam, chewing his fingernails. "He keeps me away from the rest of them, you know. I'll talk to them myself. Tonight. After the show."

"If you like," said Helen.

"Hi there." Adam stuck his head around the dressing room door, trying not to mind that the conversation instantly skittered to a halt. "How are you all doing?"

"Fine," said one of the junior troupe members cautiously. He was half-way through removing his make-up, and Adam tried not to stare at his wide red downturned mouth.

"Excellent." Adam resisted the urge to rub his hands together encouragingly. "Great show tonight, by the way."

Everyone stared at him like frightened rabbits.

"I wanted to talk to you about a proposal I've got," he went on.

The clowns drew closer together.

"It's to do with the laundry costs," he said.

"Amory deals with all of that," said a clown with a green wig and red spotted trousers. "You need to talk to him."

"Yes, I know," said Adam. "I just wondered if you'd mind sharing your thoughts on it."

"Like what?" asked the youngest member of the troupe, who was still wearing the back end of the horse costume.

"Well," said Adam, "I know we're all falling behind on pay. And I want to sort that out, I really do. And to do that, we all need the Starlight to become more profitable."

There was a brief flicker of interest from the frightened faces gazing back at him.

"Of course the gate receipts are going back up at last," said Adam. "Which is brilliant. And thank you all, by the way, for the work you've done to make that happen – I feel like I don't really thank any of you often enough…but if there's anything else we can do to save money, that's going to help too. I've got a proposal here for you all to look at. If you wouldn't mind…"

The back end of the horse held up a tentative hand, then froze. As Adam watched, he saw the blood drain from the clown's face as if someone had pulled a plug out of an artery. With a feeling of foreboding, he turned around.

"I think," said Doctor Whiteface, staring straight into Adam's eyes, "that maybe you and I ought to have a quiet conversation outside."

"Well?" said Helen.

"I don't want to talk about it," said Adam, and shut himself in his caravan.

"Can I come in and talk to you?" Adam knocked on the door of Helen's caravan, which was looking especially pretty today, with the windows sparkling and the curtains newly washed.

"As long as you take your shoes off," she said. "I've just cleaned in here."

Adam left his shoes on the steps and padded into the caravan, hoping the holes in his socks wouldn't show.

"It's Scary Doctor Whiteface, isn't it," said the Helen.

Adam nodded.

"What's the problem this time?"

"He caught me talking to the troupe without his permission," said Adam, swallowing. "It was awful. Like being back at school. He scares me to death! I don't understand what's gone wrong. I used to be strong enough for anything, and now…"

"Now you feel like you've got no energy left?"

"Yes," said Adam, amazed. "He's all I can think about. I'm being haunted by a man in white make-up and an orange wig. How did that even happen?"

"Tell me something," said Helen. "What do you think he actually wants?"

"I don't know. I don't know! I've tried everything I can think of. I thought he liked structure, so I had formal meetings with proper agendas. I thought he liked to feel in control, so I let him set the agenda items. I thought his whole objective was to get that salary increase, so I've framed everything I've showed him in terms of how it benefits his team and gets us closer to achieving that. I've tried being nice. I've tried being firm. I've tried being confrontational. I've tried being spontaneous. I've tried sharing my ideas, I've tried asking him for his ideas, I've gone to him with problems, I've gone to him with solutions. And none of it's good enough for him. None of it makes him happy. He just derails everything I do."

"Yes," said Helen.

"So what do I do?"

"What can you think of to do?"

"I can't think of anything to do," said Adam. "I have tried every single strategy I can think of. I am officially out of ideas. It's like he doesn't want anything to change at all, and instead of trying to help make things better, he's putting all his energy into making my life a misery and stopping me from getting anything done."

He looked at Helen for help, but she just looked blandly back at him.

"What do I do?" he begged.

"You don't need me to tell you. Not anymore. You've already got the answer. In fact you've already told me the answer. Now you just need to act on it."

Adam stared at her.

"Is this a joke?" Doctor Whiteface waved the agenda at Adam. Beneath the heading was a single item:

Making you happy

"Be honest," said Adam. "Do you like working for me?"

Doctor Whiteface blinked.

"Excuse me?"

"Do you like working for me?" Adam repeated.

"That's hardly important, is it? We're both professionals, there's no need for -"

"Because," said Adam, "I'm pretty sure you don't."

Doctor Whiteface bristled.

"Well, I like to think I can get on with anyone -"

"Of course you can," Adam lied smoothly. "You're a very intelligent businessman. But this isn't about what you *can* do. It's about what you'd *like* to do."

It was the first time he'd ever seen his adversary silenced.

"I said ages ago that I want to make everyone happier at work," Adam said, "and I know I've made a lot of changes that really aren't working for you. Are they?"

"…no." The word came out reluctantly, but it was out.

"I thought not. And I know I'm going to lose you eventually, because you're very talented and there are plenty of other circuses and it's only a matter of time before you tell me someone's poached you for their outfit instead. Probably at a higher salary than you're getting now."

The other man's face was a frantic blank.

"So rather than keep you in a job you're not enjoying until you find the right position, and both of us being at each other's throats the whole time, I thought we could come to an arrangement."

"Did you, now?"

"Yes."

There was a short pause while everyone considered this.

"You can't fire me," said Doctor Whiteface at last. "I've kept to the absolute letter of my contract, there's no way you can -"

"Absolutely not. This isn't about performance, and no-one will ever say it is. This is about what's right for you." He stood up. "Shall we meet again tomorrow to talk about how we might move forward?"

"With what kind of package?" asked Doctor Whiteface, leaning menacingly across the desk.

"Your full three months notice," said Adam. "Plus something for each year of service. Payable as a lump sum." He took a piece of paper from his pocket and passed it across the table. "I'm sure you'd like some time to consider it. The only thing I'll have to ask is that you keep this completely confidential. Obviously I can't do this for staff member who's thinking of moving on. This is strictly for, um, for, for -"

"Yes?" said Doctor Whiteface, with a gleam of malice.

Only for those people who are positively damaging to everything I'm trying to do.

"Only for long-serving team members who've made the kind of contribution you have," Adam improvised. "You'll leave quite a big void when you go, and I'd rather manage that to my timeline rather than yours. Which is why I'm happy to discuss a managed exit, rather than just waiting for your resignation letter to arrive. I'm sure you get offers."

"Damn right I do."

"So, um, I'll leave that one with you, shall I? Let me know when you're ready to talk."

"You all right, boss?" asked Gabriel, looking at Adam in concern. Adam was pacing up and down outside his caravan, staring at the ground and muttering to himself.

"Fine," said Adam, without looking up.

"What – um – do you mind me asking what you're doing?"

"Praying," said Adam, without a trace of humour.

"So," said Adam, trying to look relaxed.

"So," said Doctor Whiteface.

"What are your thoughts?"

"It's an interesting offer," Doctor Whiteface admitted, with visible reluctance.

"I'm glad you think so."

"Hang on. Don't go rushing ahead of me, please. I didn't say I was happy. I just said it's *interesting*. There are a lot of points that you'll need to do some serious work on before we even get close to a possible deal."

"Fire away," said Adam.

"First, there's the three months' salary. You haven't specified whether that would be gross or net."

"Net," said Adam.

"No."

"No?"

"Gross. Or this conversation's over."

Adam took out his calculator and undertook a convincing pantomime of working something out.

"If we can do a deal that's ready to go by the end of this week then I can go to gross," he said. "But it has to be this week."

"Why?"

"Cash flow," said Adam, poker-faced.

"I'm not going to be railroaded into a quick decision."

"I'm not trying to. If you'd rather take longer, the original deal still stands. But if you're able to make a decision by the end of this week, then I can get you what you need on the gross pay issue."

"We'll see," said Doctor Whiteface. "Next, I'm interested to hear how you plan on explaining my sudden departure to everyone else here."

This would be the most delicate part of the whole conversation, Helen had warned him. *You can't over-estimate how much pride matters to people. Even when they're walking away.*

"What sort of statement would you be comfortable with?" Adam asked.

Doctor Whiteface snorted. "I don't see how it's my job to write your statement."

"Fair enough. I've prepared a draft for you to look at. But of course we can discuss it if there's anything you're not happy with." He passed the paper over the table.

Doctor Whiteface looked at it scornfully. "If you're expecting an instant response you're going to be disappointed. Although I can already see errors." He took out his pen. "Here, look, that's wrong – and this is wrong – and that's inaccurate -"

"I'll leave that with you then, shall I?" said Adam. "And let's put in some time when we can talk again. I want to meet your needs but we need to move fast, so how are you for tomorrow?"

"It's worse than hostage negotiation," said Adam, collapsing dramatically onto the chair at the Helen's table.

"You're doing great," said Helen. "You've nearly got a deal."

"We're not even close to a deal!"

"Yes, you are. Of course he's got to posture and make it look difficult, that's just who he is. But in his heart, he doesn't want to be here, any more than you want him to be. You've finally found your common ground."

"I've had to completely rewrite this statement." Adam tried not to flinch away from the paper being waved beneath his nose. "You'll need to get it typed up properly, I haven't got time for all that. It's not even part of my job to be doing this stuff."

"We'll miss all the extra work you put in," said Adam.

"Don't get excited, I haven't signed anything yet. If you want me to meet your deadline, I'll need something else on top of what we've already discussed."

"I see," said Adam.

"You'll have to pay my plane fare. To Moscow."

Adam tried not to let his exultation show. Bendicks Circus was in Moscow.

"So," he said. "If I review this statement and check we're both happy with it, and if I can find a way to make the plane fare happen, do we have something that works for both of us and that we can put in place by the end of the week?"

"First Class," said Doctor Whiteface, in one final spasm of awkwardness.

"If I can agree to that, have we got something that works for us both?"

There was nothing left to say, nothing left he could ask for.

"You've got a deal," he said.

"So," said Adam briskly. "Any questions?"

The clown troupe were staring at him in shock. But behind the shock, he thought he could see the first glimmers of excitement.

"Who do we report to?" the back end of the horse asked at last.

"Who's next in seniority?" The front end held up a hand. "Okay, you for now, and let's see how it goes."

"Can we change the routine?" asked the one with the squirty flower.

"You've got some thoughts? Fantastic. Come and see me after the show, we'll talk about it."

"And he's really happy to be going?"

"Course he is," said the clown who drove the car. "He's spent years making us all as miserable as sin, now he gets to go and do it to some other poor devils. Oh come on, don't look at me like you weren't all thinking it too. I'm sick of driving the car, anyone fancy a swap around tonight?"

Adam closed the door quietly and slipped away.

"It was expensive," Adam admitted to Helen over the teapot.

"Did it cost more than every ounce of your time and energy, plus all the enthusiasm of the Clown troupe? Because that's what it was costing you to keep him."

"All that money, though? Just to get rid of someone who was probably going to leave anyway?"

"It was within what you decided you could live with. That makes it a good deal."

"And I don't even want to think about what Bendicks are going to make of him when he gets there -"

"He wasn't right for the Starlight. That doesn't mean he's wrong for everywhere else. He'll probably thrive there, and everyone there will think you're mad for letting him out of your clutches. But you won't mind, because you made the right decision for both of you. And now you can stop worrying, and move on to the next job that needs doing."

"You might have a point," said Adam. "But still…First Class…"

"You'll save it in three months on what you used to pay shipping that desk around the globe," said Helen.

"My God," said Adam. "I'd forgotten about that." He put down his mug. "I don't suppose you have any marshmallows, do you?"

Ten minutes later, he and a number of other performers were toasting marshmallows over the flames of a comforting oak-wood bonfire.

The New Moon Party

Adam shook his head in disbelief, and added up the numbers one more time. Then once more, just to be sure. Then once more, on general principle. And once more, just in case.

Then he closed down his spreadsheet, shut up his laptop, tidied his desk and wandered out of his caravan into thick snow and a treacly dawn light. They were in Reykjavik, and the sun was only above the horizon for a few hours a day.

"Hello," said Helen, without looking round. She was folding clothes into a suitcase, and there was a general air of confusion in her normally tidy caravan.

"We're in the black," said Adam, almost in a whisper.

"Well, of course you are. Could you hold these for me, please? Thank you."

"We're in the black," Adam repeated, over the stack of books on interpretation of the I Ching.

"And these as well? You're a star."

"I said," said Adam patiently, "we're in -"

"The black. Yes, I know. Why are you so surprised? The Starlight's a different place these days. Everyone loves

168

working here, and it shows in every performance you give. How could you not be in profit?"

"It worked," said Adam. "It actually worked."

"It always works." She opened a suitcase. "Can I have those books now? Thank you."

"Why are you packing everything?" Adam asked. "We're not moving on for another week."

Helen's smile was a little sad.

"Oh," said Adam, feeling his world rock slightly on its foundations.

"You really don't need me any more, you know," she said.

"Don't I?"

"Look how far you've come. You've taken a failing business on the verge of collapse, and turned it into a thriving place everyone's proud to be a part of. Of course you don't need me anymore."

"I just sort of thought you'd always be here," Adam said.

"There are others that need me more. But you can always get in touch." She closed the suitcase with a brisk little snap. "And in the meantime, now you actually *are* back in profit, I have a very important final task for you…"

Like all small, enclosed worlds, the Starlight Circus was in possession of a frighteningly efficient grapevine. The news of the New Moon Party was all around the team almost as soon as Adam had finished asking Anne to draw up the invitations. His memories of corporate "celebrations" was that they required months of work, cost thousands of pounds and were enjoyed by practically no-one, but the New Moon Party seemed to be organising itself. He was besieged with offers of help. Bill promised to light and decorate the Big Top; Anne was put in charge of the Beer Fund; Lola and Marcus took control of the catering.

With memories of glossy corporate conferences filling his head, Adam began drawing up lists of team building activities and organised party games, but Helen discovered them and took them firmly away. "This isn't for you, it's for them," she told him. "The only thing you're trying to achieve is for everyone to have a lovely time. Save the team building for another day."

"But that's how we always used to do it at my old place," Adam protested.

"*So?* Be different! Live a little! It'll be fine, you'll see. The best parties organise themselves."

The night of the New Moon was still and cold, with a starry sky like salt grains spilled on black silk. Wrapped in wool and velvet, the performers streamed shivering towards the pale white glow of the Big Top, lit by every spotlight the Starlight Circus possessed and looking as if someone had lassoed the moon and anchored it to the earth with guy ropes.

"What if it's rubbish?" Adam whispered to Helen as he stood nervously by the barbecue and turned over sausages.

"They're performers," she laughed. "Do you honestly think they don't know how to throw the world's best party?"

It began when Marcus bowed low to Anne and produced a bouquet of flowers from the air. When she rolled her eyes and reluctantly took them, the bouquet gave a sort of shiver and fell into pieces and Anne was suddenly holding a papier maché carousel horse that, in turn, blazed up in a jet of flame, leaving behind a blown-glass model of the dragon carousel.

"Showoff." Ted cuffed Marcus around the head.

"Sez you," said Marcus, grinning. "How's the new routine coming?"

"Brilliant. Hey, do you want to see?"

"What, right now?"

"No time like the present…"

It took Ted and Gabriel a few minutes to get the rotating board into position, by which time a number of other performers, including Adam, had gathered to watch.

"You're sure about this," said Adam, as Ted put on his blindfold.

"Very sure," said Lola, serene and upside-down. "Ready, Ted."

Drawn by the sudden tense silence, the Cossack riders drifted over to watch. The applause at the end was deafening.

"Holy shit," said Gabriel, slapping Ted on the back. "Get that man a beer." Lola cleared her throat. "And that woman as well, of course." He looked thoughtfully at the trapeze. "Hey, anyone want to see what we've been working on? It's better to music, but – oh -" the band members were quietly putting down their plates and beer-bottles. "Well, thanks - if you're sure…" Behind him, Belle and Henry were looking eager. "Oh, come on then, you two. Don't you dare fall this time."

"Um," said the Horse's Front End.

"Yeah," said the Horse's Back End.

Suddenly, the clowns had all disappeared to their make-up hut.

"What's happening?" Adam asked.

"The Greatest Show on Earth," Helen told him.

It was the best performance Adam had ever seen them give. This was the circus he remembered from his dreams, the circus where everyone ran into the ring with a smile plastered across their face, where everyone's costume was bright and beautiful, where performers clustered eagerly in the wings and exchanged excited whispers as they waited for their turn to share their latest and their best, where every act over ran and nobody cared.

It didn't matter that the audience consisted of him and Helen, or that no-one had paid to see it happen. This performance wasn't about anyone's day-jobs. This was a group of people doing exactly what they wanted. Showing off for each other. Cheering each other on. Having fun. Doing what they loved best in the world.

He stood in the wings and watched them, and knew that if he lived as long as his grandfather and died at a hundred and two, he'd never forget this moment.

When the band played the final flourish, and everyone gathered around the barbecue, sweaty and exhausted and ready to drink beer and eat sausages and dance until the sun rose again at noon, he wondered if he ought to say something, to summarise what had just happened, to recognise what they had achieved. But he couldn't think of a single thing to say that wouldn't sound cheesy and ridiculous, and also he wasn't sure he could speak through the lump in his throat; so he just kept quiet and began flipping burgers.

But that was okay, he thought happily. Sometimes, life at the Top was about knowing when to keep quiet, enjoy the moment, and open another beer.

Appendix

So, how was it for you? We hope we've whetted your appetite for putting the principles of Employee Engagement into practice, and delivering a stronger bottom line performance as a result.

"Tough at the Top" is a light-hearted introduction to some of the key principles of Employee Engagement, but there's plenty of hard science and research behind every single one of them. Engaged employees build stronger, more profitable businesses with higher growth, lower staff turnover and stronger performances on just about every single business metric.

Here's a chapter by chapter reminder of the key principles we've explored.

Chapter One – The Dream

We all know what a good business looks like. Growing turnover, healthy profit margins, happy customers...and employees who love working there. But which comes first? Does success drive engagement, or does engagement drive success?

Study after study has demonstrated that engagement predicts success far better than success predicts engagement. It's perfectly possible for a business to deliver excellent short-term results with a relatively disengaged workforce. However, low engagement levels are like a canary in a mine – being highly correlated with a significantly poorer long-term performance.

Chapter Two – The Reality

Struggling business; unhappy workforce. Which do you focus on first? It may seem counter intuitive to say "Focus on your people rather than your numbers", but the simple fact is that none of us can fix a struggling business entirely on our own. If your people aren't engaged with what you're trying to achieve, your chances of getting there are drastically reduced. On the other hand, when everyone in your team is united behind a strong common purpose, success becomes significantly more likely.

The one tempting factor that numbers have in their favour is that they are, by definition, extremely measurable. That's why switched on businesses of all shapes and sizes are not only using robust, well-proven techniques to measure and monitor how engaged their employees are. They are proactively doing something with the information that they gather and developing internal communication and engagement strategies to increase the level of employee engagement.

Chapter Three – The Vision Thing

Do you have a company vision, mission and values? If so, how do you use them? Do they drive how you and your team behave? Or are they just some nice sounding words you all read once, and then put in a drawer? And how does it make your employees feel when you commit to being 'progressive and forward looking', but don't live up to it in practice?

A company's vision needs to be built and crafted with the active support and input of the whole team. When everyone has the same understanding of where the company's going and why it's worth being part of that journey, you've laid the foundations for creating truly engaged employees.

Chapter Four - The Cossack Riders

There's an old joke about a General Manager who's trying to work out how to stop his staff leaving for his competitors. After much thought, he finally finds the solution...he's going to convert his entire workforce to badly trained idiots who no-one in their right mind would ever want to employ.

Of course, that doesn't mean you have to let your employees go without a fight. But the way to win the retention battle isn't to put a stop to development opportunities – it's to find ways to develop them that also works for you. Training opportunities are a perquisite for high levels of employee engagement. It sends the message out loud and clear that the organisation has a genuine interest in employee well-being and personal development.

Chapter Five – The Cleaner

When you find someone who's fantastically good at their job, it's often tempting to try to reward them with what you perceive to be a higher status, more exciting job. Sometimes, that's exactly the right thing to do - but not always. How do you manage and reward the teacher who's brilliant in the classroom? The researcher who excels on the lab bench? The receptionist who makes every visitor feel welcome?

Making sure your experts know they're valued without taking them away from their field of expertise requires a different approach. It's important to ensure that your progression and reward programmes accommodate high value experts who want to remain in their post long-term, as well as ambitious high-fliers who want to climb to the top of the pyramid. Personal recognition is much more powerful as a longer term motivator than bonuses or other financial rewards.

Chapter Six – The Carousel

Very often people have excellence in areas that are not exposed or demonstrated by their role. You might discover that your team members are secretly brilliant cartoonists, designers, bloggers, artists, public speakers, strategists….and so on.

By uncovering skills and core strengths – you can help employees feel more rewarded and recognised. By shaping the role to the person, rather than trying to squeeze the person into the role, you help everyone in your company to truly enjoy their work and make the most of all their talents.

Chapter Seven – The Trick Dive

Going beyond the everyday can be frightening for all of us. But with the right kind of leadership we can all be inspired to complete challenges we never knew were possible. Adam couldn't make Marcel dive off the top of the Trapeze tower… but with the right example, Marcel decided for himself that it was worth a try.

As a leader, it's your responsibility to model the kind of behaviour you want to see in your team. We are social creatures, and we often learn appropriate and valued behaviours by observing authority figures. Living out your company's values every day is a very powerful method for instilling them into your business culture.

Chapter Eight – The Tigers Are Killing Us

Many established businesses have a problem like Dmitri's tiger act – a piece of much-loved historical baggage that's holding back growth and eating up profits, but that no-one can bear to part with.

Change is rarely comfortable, and we tend to over-estimate the costs and risks of changing, and under-estimate the costs and risks of standing still. A good leader will find ways of moving the business on without breaking hearts along the way. And often on the other side of a successful change programme are people looking at each other and saying, "Why on earth didn't we do this before?"

Chapter Nine – The Odd Couple

Have you ever had to referee employees who have completely opposing perspectives? Ted and Lola see the same problem, but they are interpreting it in totally different ways – and they're both vital stakeholders in the final solution.

Good people management isn't about banging the gavel and telling everyone to get back to work. It's about understanding and valuing everyone's contribution, and finding a solution that meets everyone's needs. To do this, we need to understand and recognise that people have different desires and values. They also have different perspectives on what the problem is and what the solution might be. There is rarely a "right" or "wrong" answer.

Chapter Ten – The Accident

"To have good ideas, have a lot of them." Thomas Edison had a lot of ideas – some of them brilliant, but quite a lot of them a bit rubbish. It's a simple mathematical truth that the more often we innovate, the more often we'll fail.

In a tough economic climate (or sometimes even in a comfortable one), it's easy to panic about the costs of trying and failing, and to ignore the risk of standing still. But our job as leaders isn't to stamp out failure. It's to give our employees the freedom and confidence to fail without fear.

If you don't have any failures – you're not trying hard enough.

Chapter Eleven – Send In The Clowns

At some point in every manager's career, we'll encounter an employee who simply isn't right for our company. No matter how hard we try, we simply can't make them fit into the culture we're trying to build. They will poison the system and those around them, channelling their negative energy into destruction rather than construction.

It's not a situation many of us would find pleasant - and it's not an easy one to manage, but there are techniques that can make the parting smoother and less painful for everyone concerned. Don't be afraid to seek specialist advice – it's not a sign of weakness or defeat on either side. If you let the situation continue unchallenged it's not fair on you, the other team members, the organisation or indeed the individual themselves.

Chapter Twelve – The New Moon Party

We said at the start that employee engagement predicts business success far more strongly than business success predicts employee engagement. It's so important that we thought we'd say it again. The Starlight Circus's success is driven by the individual performance of every employee in it. When they sharpen up their acts, success becomes almost inevitable.

When developing a rewards and incentives programme, it's amazing how many managers never think to ask the people they're supposedly rewarding what they'd actually like. Senior Leaders spend thousands of pounds on overseas conferences, and then are bewildered when employees complain about giving up a weekend with their families to spend two days in a destination they didn't choose, to listen to motivational speeches from senior management. Try not to confuse "motivation" with "reward". If you're not sure what people would like, ask them.

And don't worry if you get a number of different answers. The best incentive programmes – like the best managers – are always flexible.

H&H

Communications – People – Branding

Hesslewood Hall Business Centre
Ferriby Road
Hessle
East Yorkshire
HU13 0LH

talktous@handhcomms.co.uk
01482 222 230